"O'Hara helps us find the quiet place inside us where inner peace abounds. In our harried lives, it's comforting to remember the quiet place can be revisited." —Michele Weiner-Davis, M.S.W.,
author of *Fire Your Shrink* and *Divorce Busting*

"With simple, inspiring advice, Nancy O'Hara shows us how to bring awareness to the thousand and one challenges of daily life."
—Robert Gerzon,
author of *Finding Serenity in an Age of Anxiety*

"A wise book. . . . O'Hara's elegance as a writer is matched by her elegance as a thinker." —Betsy Lerner,
author of *Food and Loathing: A Lament*

"This simple yet profound book ought to be read by all people who live in the so-called civilized world. Civilization has deprived us of our natural condition as human beings. Nancy O'Hara offers a guide to the natural, peaceful world.

"Even just reading the chapter titles is worthwhile: 'Let Your Breathing Guide You,' 'Make It a Habit,' 'Keep It Yours,' 'Turn Bad Situations to Your Advantage,' 'When Things Don't Go Your Way.' These phrases can stimulate our sincere curiosity. In our busy everyday life, we do not pay much attention to these simple matters, hence no quiet corner. As the author says about attention, 'It is truly simple and immediately rewarding.'" —Eido T. Shimano,
Abbot of the Zen Studies Society
Dai Bosatsu Zendo

"There is breathtaking wisdom and strength to be found in a single moment of silence—and Nancy O'Hara offers a kind invitation to listen. *Find a Quiet Corner* is a gentle opening; it beckons us into fruitful practice. Here, we harvest the compelling grace that is born only in the quiet of our lives."

—Wayne Muller, minister and therapist,
author of *Thursday's Child: The Spiritual Advantages of a Painful Childhood*

Find a Quiet Corner

ALSO BY NANCY O'HARA

Just Listen: A Guide to Finding Your Own True Voice

Zen by the Brush: A Japanese Painting and Meditation Set
(illustrations by Seiko Susan Morningstar)

3 Bowls: Vegetarian Recipes
from an American Zen Buddhist Monastery
(with Seppo Ed Farrey)

Work from the Inside Out: 7 Steps to Loving What You Do

Find a Quiet Corner

INNER PEACE:

ANYTIME,

ANYWHERE

Nancy O'Hara

STERLING

New York / London

www.sterlingpublishing.com

Sterling and the distinctive Sterling logo are registered trademarks
of Sterling Publishing Co., Inc.

Library of Congress Cataloging-in-Publication Data
O'Hara, Nancy.
Find a quiet corner : inner peace, anytime, anywhere / Nancy O'Hara.
p. cm.
Originally published: New York : Warner Books, c1995.
Includes index.
ISBN 978-1-4027-6576-6
1. Stress (Psychology) 2. Stress management. 3. Peace of mind. I. Title.
BF575.S75O27 2008
158'.1082—dc22
2008039525

10 9 8 7 6 5 4 3 2 1

Published by Sterling Publishing Co., Inc.
387 Park Avenue South, New York, NY 10016
Material in this book based on text published
in *Find a Quiet Corner* ©1995 Nancy O'Hara and
Serenity in Motion ©2003 Nancy O'Hara
© 2009 by Nancy O'Hara
Distributed in Canada by Sterling Publishing
c/o Canadian Manda Group, 165 Dufferin Street
Toronto, Ontario, Canada M6K 3H6
Distributed in the United Kingdom by GMC Distribution Services
Castle Place, 166 High Street, Lewes, East Sussex, England BN7 1XU
Distributed in Australia by Capricorn Link (Australia) Pty. Ltd.
P.O. Box 704, Windsor, NSW 2756, Australia

Manufactured in the United States
All rights reserved

Design and layout by Debbie Glasserman

Sterling ISBN 978-1-4027-6576-6

For information about custom editions, special sales, premium and
corporate purchases, please contact Sterling Special Sales
Department at 800-805-5489 or specialsales@sterlingpublishing.com.

To Dad, Donge, and Michael

Acknowledgments

With a deep sense of gratitude I bow to all my teachers, bod-hisattvas, and friends. Calling out a few by name, I want to express my thanks to Mom and Dad, first and foremost, for my life then and now; my siblings, who continue to help me learn about unconditional love: Jan, Mike, Bill, Colleen, Karen, Kathy, and Rick; and my extended family, who have supported and guided me in my spiritual recovery: Bill, Bob, Lois, Barbara Suter, and Boun Nancy Berg among countless others—you know who you are. To my Zen teachers and dharma brothers and sisters, who offer me a foundation that makes spiritual and practical sense: Donge John Haber who continues to live in my heart as a beacon of love and truth all these years after his physical death; Eido Shimano Roshi, a Rinzai Zen master and my teacher who carried Zen from the East to America so that we could all benefit from its wisdom; Seigan Ed Glassing, a true Zen monk and good friend; all of you with whom I've sat zazen, sesshin after sesshin, sit after sit; and all my students and read-ers—you give me the courage and faith to continue.

I also want to thank David Nelson for being a friend and for believing that *Quiet Corner* and *Serenity* deserved a second life in print.

And last but not least I bow deeply to Michael Levine, my intimate partner, friend, and truest teacher. You support me in more ways than you know.

I look forward to many more years with all of you.

Contents

PART II: SERENITY IN MOTION— INNER PEACE, ANYTIME, ANYWHERE 91

Preface

Twenty years ago this year, burdened with a once-again broken heart, I took my first step into a Zen Buddhist monastery. I met my first Zen monk, who would help me change my life. I sat down on a round, black meditation cushion, and confronted myself and my deep pain for the first time ever in my thirty-eight years. I took a deep breath and then exhaled fully, which I hadn't done for a very long time.

There were a lot of firsts that year, twenty years ago, when my life as I knew it derailed and I began the search for new tracks to set it on. It took a few years, three exactly, for one more huge life implosion to set me firmly on the path I've followed ever since—a path that has challenged me, excited me, calmed me, scared me, and given me deep inner peace; a path that ever so slowly has moved me away from the mental torment and excruciating internal pain that I had become accustomed to and thought was my fate to carry; a path that has sometimes gently, sometimes not so gently, taken me into the light.

I will turn fifty-eight this year and the firsts continue: I am in an intimate partnership—the first to last seven years—that gets better every day. I finished writing my first novel—a once well-hidden dream secret. My first book, *Find a Quiet Corner*, is being granted a second life, and my most recent book, *Serenity in Motion*, is being republished with it.

These two combined books in your hands represent the bookends of my spiritual life for the past twenty years, and I am thrilled that they are now joined together in one volume. It's as if the two halves of my brain, of my heart, and of my entire being have finally merged into one, with the marriage of these two books representing the outer manifestation of my internal search and harmony.

It signifies that maybe, just maybe, after twenty years of practice, I am beginning to have an inkling of what it means to *be*. As I look forward to the next twenty years of this mysterious life, I wonder (without expectation—and that is my greatest lesson learned and practiced!) what new insights are in store for me, what the world will look like, and what more I can do to serve others.

Buddhism, which is called the *Middle Way*, has been the vehicle through which I have experienced selfless moments. And at this time, as I contemplate my life and feel deep gratitude about the course it has taken, a Christian prayer comes to my mind as a reminder that it's not about Buddhism or Christianity or this God or that one; it's about love, kindness, and compassion for ourselves and others. This is all that matters, however we learn it.

This prayer, by St. Francis of Assisi, goes like this:
Lord, make me a channel of thy peace—that where there is hatred, I may bring love—that where there is wrong, I may bring the spirit of forgiveness—that where there is discord, I may bring harmony—that where there is error, I may bring truth—that where there is doubt, I may bring faith—that where there is despair, I may bring hope—that where there are shadows, I may bring light—that where there is sadness, I may bring joy. Lord, grant that I may seek rather to comfort than to be comforted—to understand, than to be understood—to love, than to be loved. For it is by self-forgetting that one finds. It is by forgiving that one is forgiven. It is by dying that one awakens to Eternal Life. Amen.

...

Each time I read this prayer aloud, if I concentrate and truly listen, tears come to my eyes. It awakens in me a deep caring and offers up the possibility that perfect loving is possible. I believe this prayer. I believe it to be an authentic product of love. It soothes and comforts me with its promise of enlightenment. Since stepping on my spiritual path, I've tasted some of what this prayer offers, I've learned to forgive myself each time I realize how imperfect I am, and I accept that I am perfect in my imperfection.

This brings me to a passage that I found in a Zen text twenty years ago, which I wrote on an index card and set on my desk so that I could be reminded every day what I was seeking and where it might be found. It's a message that continues to resonate deep in my gut and promises me that what I seek is not only possible, but truly simple: *The essence of Buddhism is no more than living in harmony with the changing circumstances of one's life, without strain or compulsion.*

I never wrote down which text this came from or who wrote it, so I apologize to the author for not giving proper credit here. I had no idea then how profound and lasting this message would be for me. I now realize that if the only thing I've learned over the past twenty years is how to live this way, then that is all the knowing I need. And if you can take away just one small gem from this book that inspires and supports you on your spiritual path, then the circle will be complete.

As I read through *Find a Quiet Corner* and *Serenity in Motion* to determine what I might want to change, omit, or expand upon for this new combined edition, I realized that if I were to write either of these books today, they would be different. But I also appreciate that they are perfect just as they are and that they represent my heart-mind as it was when I wrote them and therefore should be left untouched. So I offer them to you basically as they were initially conceived and hope that they will guide you toward your true self, into your quiet corner, and then out into the world—with serenity and inner peace.

JULY 2008, NEW YORK CITY

Part I

Find a Quiet Corner

A SIMPLE GUIDE

TO SELF-PEACE

Introduction

I used to wish my life away. I lived my life thinking ahead to the next thing—the next day, when I had a date with so-and-so and wouldn't that be nice; the next job, because I hated my current one so much; the next year, when I was planning to take that great vacation, which held the promise of changing my life; the next prince charming, who would rescue me from my life because the last one was really a frog and I was meant to be saved. I couldn't wait for the next experience that was sure to transform me and my life. I still have the tendency to live in the future, but today I notice when I do and am usually able to catch myself and bring my attention back to the moment. But it took some time and a lot of pain to shift my awareness into the present.

My journey in search of a quiet corner began with loss and a great deal of despair. It was 1985. I was living my life as usual, waiting for something to happen, retreating from myself and my world with drugs and alcohol, and living in a black hole of despair, not caring much about my life. In fact, I considered ending my life just to escape the misery. And then my father died. The shock of losing the only person in my life who seemed to love me was devastating. For a short while, I sank further into despair and a haze of intoxication. But for some reason, his death made it clear to me that I wanted to live. I saw how I was slowly slipping into oblivion. Some force beyond me and my ego drove me to admit that my life was a mess, and I made a decision to move toward life rather than death. I put down drugs and alcohol and began the move toward health.

Three years later, after spending much time working

toward recovery, another loss forced me to recommit to my quiet-corner journey. My prince charming of the moment left me, for seemingly no reason. My mind wouldn't leave me alone. My ego was crushed, my heart was bruised, and my mind blamed me. I sank into a self-deprecating state of loneliness and tortured myself with notions that it was all my fault, that I was unlovable, that I would never be happy, and that I got what I deserved. The pain was debilitating, and I sometimes thought I might drop off the sane world into that of the insane. That's how noisy and confused my mind was. Because I was desperate, I went on a retreat to a Zen Buddhist monastery in the Catskill Mountains. Because I always wanted to be the good student and get the gold star at the end of the day, I did what was suggested that weekend. When told to sit still during *zazen* (seated meditation in Zen Buddhism), I sat still. I was in so much mental pain that I would have done anything for the promise of soothing it.

The physical pain of sitting was so excruciating I was convinced that I was doing serious permanent damage to my body. But something happened that weekend in the stillness of sitting and in the encounter with pain. The physical pain took my mind off the mental pain and taught me that pain is only temporary and often simply a measure of my ego and its attachments. I continued sitting after leaving the mountain, and I went on other retreats over the next few years. My life was changing, I was changing, and the pain of that time subsided to the point where I was actually enjoying my life. By 1991, I was in a job that I loved and in a relationship that was working and I had just purchased my first home. Life was okay.

Then the bottom fell out again. Within a month, I lost my boyfriend and my job. I hadn't realized until I lost them how much my identity was wrapped up in both, especially my job.

I was a very sad and broken person. The self-blaming demons returned. I didn't know what to do next, so I retreated to the monastery for a weekend to think about my next move. Beginning with that weekend and with the help of many people, I started on yet another path of recovery. I had always wanted to write, and when I put forth the idea of spending more time at the monastery and writing about the experience, I was encouraged to do so by the monks and by many friends who cared about me. I lived there for five months and am changed from that experience.

Find a Quiet Corner is a product of all this experience. It comes from much personal pain and the need to quiet my mind. My pattern had been not to make changes in my life unless I was in great pain and my back was up against the wall. My instinct is to continue to resist change, but today I am aware when I do this and I use the techniques in this book to accept the change that is inevitable. I am grateful that my life was filled with so much pain and that I was introduced to a form of meditation that helps me to accept and understand this pain.

While you can open to any page in this book and find inspiration, you will get the most from it by working through it from front to back, from beginning to end. I know many people who are in pain and could benefit from the suggestions in this book. If I am able to help but one other person, all my pain will have been worthwhile. But I also know that we each have our own path and unless we're ready to surrender, nothing can force us. Pain is a fact of life. Joy is available to us also, but not unless we understand the pain. I have experienced joy for the first time in my life since starting on the quiet-corner path. I will continue to experience pain, but I now know that joy is also probable if I continue my quiet-corner practice.

Why a Quiet Corner?

This book is for those of you who haven't the time to do all those things that are expected of you every day. You've got the demands of your boss, the demands of your spouse, the demands of your children, the demands of your community, and perhaps most of all, the demands of your own personal making weighing on you. You are distracted to the point of mild insanity. You hardly have time to eat—how can you be expected to read a book, let alone find some alone time for yourself?

If you take a moment out of your hectic day and settle down with this book, you'll learn how to find some time and you'll get back in touch with your understanding of how important it is to spend some time with yourself. This book is not about adding yet one more burden to your already full-to-exploding life. It's about learning how to unburden yourself, how to undo some of the complications in your life and clear a path toward smoothness. While thinking of the greater good may only be a distraction just now, consider this for a moment: If our culture is to evolve, it is imperative that we each learn to take some time for ourselves on a daily basis and develop our own individual spiritual awareness. Finding a quiet corner is one way for each of us to do our part.

But the greater gain is secondary. The primary gain will be in your daily life. And it won't take a revolution or a complete change of lifestyle to enjoy the rewards. It will take only a few small movements to reap big changes.

If you've read this far, you are already aware of your need to slow down. If you feel compelled to go further, you've already accepted this. And if you read on, you'll learn some actions you can take to introduce some calmness into your life.

What Is a Quiet Corner?

A moment in time, a place in time, a breath. A quiet corner can be found anywhere, can be created anytime. It is an attitude, an outlook. It can be found in your particular approach to your particular day. A quiet corner simply needs a slight shift in perspective to emerge.

A quiet corner is the calm after a storm. Think of a morning after a snowstorm, your world buried under a foot or two of snow. Venturing outside, you may notice the effects of this blanket of white. Before the roads are plowed and cars dug out, there is no traffic noise. Most people, while perhaps dreading the shovel, are smiling and awed by the beauty of it all. You might think more carefully about each step you take. Once you've given in to this force of nature, you are in the moment aware only of your next move, not thinking of tomorrow. You can't take your usual path; you must rethink things. Your perspective shifts. You are in a quiet corner.

But it needn't take a dramatic act of nature to create a quiet corner. Once you identify this state of grace, you can learn to create it on your own. All it takes is a decision and a resignation. Give up your usual practices, leave at the door of your quiet corner all expectations, and be prepared to enter a world where anything is possible.

Breathing

This is where it all begins—and ends. The foundation of any quiet corner is breathing. If you breathe into your quiet corner and allow your breathing to direct you in your search, it will create space and quiet for your corner. As I concentrate on breathing slowly, my focus shifts and I welcome the ensuing calm as it enfolds and comforts me.

Most of us breathe very shallowly. We only breathe into our throats and don't allow oxygen deep into our bodies. Take a moment. Become aware of how you're breathing in this moment. Is your breathing deep and calm? Or is it shallow and hurried? The next time you feel stressed, panicked, or otherwise pressured, again notice your breathing patterns. Your breathing will be shallower than normal. Or you may discover that you are actually holding your breath, not breathing at all. This is a common response to stress. Think for a moment about what this might mean to your well-being.

As a simple exercise, take a breath through your nostrils and send this breath into your lower chest. Continue inhaling as you first fill up your lower chest, then your middle chest, and then your upper chest. Slowly release this breath—first the upper chest, then the middle chest, and then the lower chest. Do this three times as slowly as possible. In doing this, you will discover your first quiet corner.

If you take three deep breaths a few times during each day, especially at those critically stressful moments, you'll be on your way to reducing stress and introducing some serenity into your life. It is truly simple and immediately rewarding.

Caring about and for Yourself

As our society has become so enthralled with narcissism, many of us have come to believe that self-love is bad and selfish. We have done ourselves wrong here. There is nothing wrong with loving ourselves. In fact, this is necessary before we can truly love another. Let's try to put aside the old myths and have faith that love sent in any direction is positive and healthy.

If you've ever been on an airplane, you'll remember being told to put on your own oxygen mask in the event of an emergency before helping young children; if you help yourself first, you'll be better equipped to help others. In the same way, love yourself first. Take some time for yourself. Consider these actions to be done in the service of others. A quiet, loving corner can be the nurturing ground for your own and your family's well-being.

Love is what we all ultimately seek, but to get love, we must give it. And in order to give it, we need to know it for ourselves. Unless we take good care of ourselves, we will have nothing to give others. Caring for ourselves is the first step in the process.

Become the Person You Already Are

If you have children or have been around children, you'll notice that they are often quite content and satisfied to exist in their own little world, fascinated with the particular project that at any given moment absorbs them. Whether they are playing with building blocks or digging in the sand, for a certain amount of time they need no one and want nothing. They are comfortable in their own skin and often seem to be transported to another world.

As we become adults and assume responsibilities in the world, we tend to stop this practice; we become other- and outer-directed and relegate all childhood activities to the past. When these childlike inclinations are stifled, we lose the sense of wonderment that often accompanies them. Our creativity becomes boxed up, and we wonder why life has become dull. That child is still within us, though, and can be rediscovered in our quiet corner. It is there that we can once again get in touch with our true spirit.

Visit a neighborhood playground or ball field and watch children as they play. Volunteer to coach a Little League team, or just observe the kids as they play and let them coach you. Allow them to teach you what it's like to be free and uninhibited. After a snowfall, make a snowman with the neighborhood kids or engage in an innocent snowball fight. Ride the waves at the ocean and delight in the freedom of it. Rake leaves into a big enough pile to hide in and have some fun. As you loosen up and begin to discover how to let go and be spontaneous, take this attitude with you into your quiet corner and nurture it there. Before long, your true nature will reveal itself and some of the tension in your life will disappear.

Get to Know Yourself Again

Most of us can't remember sitting in rapture as a child. Or if we can remember, we merely mourn the loss of such times and consider them over and done with. To alter our "grown-up" way of seeing, we simply need the key of willingness.

Be willing to spend time alone with yourself. Look closely at who you are, what makes you laugh or cry. Let go of old encrusted notions that bog you down. Ease them out of your mind. Invite your idiosyncrasies to have their say, and keep the ones that thrill you.

As you spend more time with yourself, your view of the world will begin to change. You'll see yourself in a new light and have a new understanding of who you are in the world. Long-forgotten parts of you will rise to the surface and come alive. You'll be more involved in your life than ever before, thanks to your own quiet corner.

Trust in the Process

Whenever you are stuck, breathe. If you find yourself moving too fast, breathe. As you face an important decision, breathe. Breathing is crucial to your emotional and spiritual health. Whenever there is a question in your mind about what to do next or how to do it, just breathe. Sooner or later, the solution will appear. While we'd all like it sooner, we may find that later is more often the rule. And that's what makes this so hard. So many of us never give later a chance. But later always comes, if it's not sooner. So breathe and trust in the process.

Finding Your Quiet Corner

Tension and stress have an impact on our breathing, and our breath often stops at our diaphragms. We are literally cut in half by this manner of breathing, as a significant area of our body gets no oxygen. You can easily correct this and learn to breathe deep into your body, sending oxygen to your whole being. Begin with the three-part deep-breathing exercises, sending your breath deep into your abdomen. As you exhale each breath, begin to count each exhalation. Focus on your breathing and nothing else.

Inhale slowly and gradually, filling up each section of your chest. Count as you exhale, and let each count last the length of your exhalation: *o-o-o-on-n-n-ne-e.* Now slowly inhale again and on the next exhalation, count two. Again. Inhale. Exhale. Count three. This is all it takes to begin the process. Practice this three-part, three-breath breathing every day. If you can, practice throughout the day. As you read this, remember to breathe.

When breathing remains shallow, resistance to change rises and the search for a quiet corner may never begin. Practice your breathing. You will open up. Your world will open up. You'll find corners where there once was nothing. Your awareness of your surroundings will heighten. Your outlook will change. Breathe slowly and deeply.

For a while, you may only find the time to practice your breaching. That's okay. It's a beginning and it's calming and will lead to peace. If you are determined, your day will soon open up to include more. So breathe away.

Be Creative

If your creative activity has slowed down or become dormant over time, you can slowly start nurturing it back to life as you seek your quiet corner. In fact, you'll need to engage and develop your creative juices, because even though your quiet corner may be right in front of you, you'll just continue to trip over it and ignore it until you become willing to see it and use it. Creativity comes into play and touches on all aspects of your quiet corner.

Play is a key word here. Approach your quiet corner as you would your own personal playground. You know yourself better than anyone; you know what works best for you, what inspires and stimulates you. As your creativity reawakens, encourage it and feed it. Try not to approach your quiet corner as a chore, something that you must do to achieve something, even if that something is joy and harmony. Try to approach your quiet corner in a playful manner. Think of it as a break for enjoyment rather than work. Try not to edit your thoughts as you begin. Let your imagination run wild and nurture your creative mind. We all have creative minds, and it is in your quiet corner that you can retrieve yours.

One of my quiet corners came to me in a dream. The time before, during, and after sleep is my quiet-corner creative-thinking time. I'm relaxed enough to hear my right brain and willing enough to listen.

Go gently. Let go and trust yourself as you learn to explore your creative instincts.

Morning

Early morning is the perfect time to begin looking for your quiet corner. Getting up fifteen minutes to a half hour earlier than usual will give you plenty of time to spend on this new journey. And being awake before the rest of your world will add a new and peaceful dimension to your day. Simply by changing your normal patterns, your perspectives will shift. Try waking early as a new routine for a week. Then decide if it's the right time for your quiet corner.

If morning becomes you, the gifts waiting for you at that time of day will quickly penetrate your awareness. Sound changes dramatically in the early morning; light and shadows are uniquely displayed. Both inside and outside the home everything is different. People sounds are softer as the world belongs to other life. Taking a slow stroll through your neighborhood, you can hear the musical chattering of birds. Walking to a nearby park, you can listen to the wind stirring the treetops. Sit by the water. As you breathe in the soothing quiet of early morning, you'll enter your day with a new measure of calm.

Schedule a Meeting with Yourself

Although our days get so jam-packed with activity, we always seem to be able to squeeze in one more thing: a meeting with the boss or a special client, an interview with our child's teacher or caregiver, a lunch or dinner date with a special friend. Somehow we manage to get things done even though a nagging voice at the back of our brains often tells us we should do more, more, more.

Try to fit yourself into your day. Consider this appointment with yourself as your most critical one and change it only in a dire emergency. Write it in your date book, even. Be careful, though, not to choose the most difficult time for yourself. Setting yourself up to miss this most important appointment will only lead to discouragement and delay. One day at a time, decide that you are the most important date on your calendar.

Taking time for yourself is life-affirming. It will teach you that anything is possible if you continue the practice. This is just the beginning.

Physical Spaces

Certain places can have amazing power over us. Anyone would agree that the Grand Canyon is a perfect place to sit in rapt silence and soak up nature's majesty. There are few places as grand as the canyon, but our environment, no matter how grand, affects us. In searching for your quiet corner, be sensitive to a space that in and of itself produces calmness.

If you're lucky enough to have a spare room at home to designate as yours, reserve it and use it exclusively as your quiet corner. Or simply assign a corner of another room (the den, the dining room, the bedroom) and transform it into your own personal quiet corner. Include your family in this process. They might even be happy to free up some space for your corner when they see the effect it has on you. Perhaps a quiet corner could be established for each member of your family and a certain time of the day designated as quiet time for all.

If you can't find a space at home to call your own, there are many other places you can use. The back of a church when there's no service going on can be a perfect space to find your quiet corner. Before work, at lunchtime, or at the end of the day, walk into a neighborhood church, synagogue, temple, or mosque and decide if your quiet corner waits for you there.

You needn't always seek out the same place. But it does help to have one special place for those times when you have no extra energy for the search and are simply in need of some calmness. After a while, you'll be able to transform almost any space and retreat to the quiet corner in your mind.

Avoidance

As you begin to seek out your quiet corner and experiment with various options, you may hit a wall now and then. This is the wall of avoidance. It will seem to come from nowhere and will have great strength and persistence. It will tell you that this whole exercise is foolish, that you haven't the time for such things, that you have more important things to do, that you can do it tomorrow, and so on.

It's very normal to hit this wall. Although you may be convinced that a quiet corner is exactly what you need to find some balance in your life, it will take some persistence and determination on your part to succeed in finding your corner and holding on to it. Try hard not to allow the negative, dissuasive voices to win. But don't be surprised when they come. Just accept them. Keeping your determination to find your quiet corner is all that matters. Believe it or not, the avoidance voices will soon disappear altogether and be replaced by positive, encouraging voices, assuring you that you're on the right path as you seek your quiet corner.

Lunch Break

While you may be the type to eat on the run, at your desk or not at all, the lunch hour is an ideal time to set aside for your quiet corner. Even if you have Scrooge for a boss, or if you are your own Scrooge, no one will begrudge you time off to eat. While you shouldn't deny yourself a meal, there should be plenty of time to eat and spend time in your corner.

If you're really pressed for time, you can use eating as your quiet-corner activity. Most of us talk, read, or work as we eat lunch, mindlessly feeding ourselves, paying no attention at all to the activity of eating. One quiet corner you could gain during the day is to close your office door, turn off the radio, turn off the phone, and pay attention to the ritual of eating. Do nothing else. Just eat. Think about your meal and how it tastes; chew mindfully, savoring each bite. Relaxation and satisfaction will be the rewards of this truly rich quiet corner that's open to all of us.

If you're allowed time in the middle of the day to do more than just eat, you can add yet another quiet corner at this time. You could continue sitting quietly in your office; you could walk to a nearby park or a holy place, taking your lunch with you; or you could take a walk each day in a different direction, exploring the surrounding neighborhoods. No matter where you end up, remember to breathe, especially once you've found your quiet corner.

Environment

As you search for your quiet corner, your world will begin to expand and you'll notice things that have been around all along. The empty lot on the corner teeming with wildflowers or the morning church bells may enter your consciousness for the first time.

What is your most receptive sense? Are you distracted and annoyed by unnaturally loud noises? Do you feel your body relax when at the ocean? If so, be on the lookout for an especially silent spot. Do you notice a friend's perfume? Do you volunteer to mow the lawn so that you'll be the first to enjoy the smell of freshly cut grass? Your sensitivities can direct you as you proceed in selecting a corner or two. Perhaps your local park has a bed of roses you can park yourself next to so as to satisfy your visual and olfactory senses. If you loved the stillness of libraries as a child, you might try your neighborhood library for a hushed environment. Create your own environment and include elements that speak directly to you.

There are certain times of the day that imbue almost any place with a sense of holiness. It's the place in time that becomes special. For instance, sunrise or sunset can create an atmosphere that exists at no other time. Even special places have a time during the day when they become enhanced and more special than usual. Be on the lookout for this magical confluence of time and place.

As you continue to observe your surroundings and register your responses to their stimuli, your choices will become endless. Remaining alert and aware will broaden your reach. As you open up, so will your world.

Find the Time

Desire is the only requirement necessary to find the time. But find the time we must. Otherwise, all intention of finding a quiet corner will remain in our heads as just another good idea. Probably one-quarter of my memory bank was filled with such notions—creative ideas that sat idly by waiting for me to take some action. Little by little, though, as I spend time in my quiet corner (one idea I had a strong enough desire to liberate), I am examining each of these old ideas, resurrecting some, quietly laying others to rest—doing some housecleaning of my crowded mind.

If you feed your desire to spend some time in your own quiet corner, you will find the time. Ten minutes here, twenty minutes there. Before you know it, as you get back in touch with yourself and your mind begins to clear, you'll look forward to the fifteen minutes at the end of your workday that you've set aside for yourself. And you'll begin to find other chunks of time waiting for you.

Clichés stand the test of time because of the truth nestled in them. One cliché comes to mind here: "Where there's a will, there's a way." You could also say, "Where there's desire, there's time for a quiet corner."

Solitude

If you're unaccustomed to spending time alone, it will take some time to adjust to the idea and then to the experience of aloneness. Solitude need not be lonely. In fact, as you learn how to spend your time, a sense of richness within you will develop and any problem of feeling alone will fade away. You'll become absorbed in your activity, and the outside world will cease to exist. Outside pressures will quiet down, and the demands put on you by yourself and others will subside. When you return to your world, you'll have a fuller appreciation of the people in your life and more love in your heart.

You might flinch at the idea of spending time alone. Perhaps your memories of time spent alone are sad ones associated with loneliness. Or maybe you're the type who loves to be surrounded by people, and when no one's around, the TV or radio will be on just for the company. Instead of thinking your quiet corner will take you away from others, think of being alone in your quiet corner as a means of bringing you closer to the people in your life. This outlook might make your quiet corner easier to face at first. After some time, when you realize the truth of this, you'll settle down and your resistance will gradually disappear.

The End of the Day

Put the kids to bed. Prepare for the next day in the usual manner. Then settle down to spend some time in your quiet corner. This period, after the rest of your world has retired for the day, is another perfect time to create a corner. This time of day has its own unique character, and delaying your bedtime slightly will give you a chance to experience it.

The energy in the air quiets in the late evening. A stillness that exists at no other time of day hangs about. There's no need to artificially create quiet. It is waiting for you. Take advantage of it. Even if you have the energy to spend only a few minutes with yourself at this time, it is enough. Simply sit quietly and reflect on your day. Breathe in the calm that surrounds you. Think of nothing. Just breathe. As you review your day, let go of any resentments that might have come up that day. Don't blame yourself or others for difficulties; simply resolve to do better tomorrow. This is the time to nurture yourself and allow the pervasive calm to work its miracle.

It's Your Life

Some people believe that if we make a mess of this life, we'll have another chance to get it right in the next one. Others believe that we have but one life and don't get another chance. Still others believe that we'll be rewarded or punished in the afterlife for our behavior in this one. Whatever you believe is true about your future, you would probably agree that all we can be completely sure of is the present moment. This is it!

Here you are, in this life, in your life, in this moment. Why not do the best you can with what you have now? Treating yourself well in the present rewards you and the people around you immediately. If the rewards extend beyond this moment, so much the better. A quiet corner will be the perfect nurturing ground for reaping the rewards of your life, now or later.

If You Think You Already Spend Too Much Time Alone

There's a thin line between solitude and isolation, between solitude and loneliness. The quality of the time spent alone separates the one from the other. We are social animals. We need the company of other people. Too much time spent unconnected can be unhealthy, especially if we dwell on the fact of our aloneness. On the other hand, never spending any time on our own can engulf us in crushing lonesomeness.

Balance is crucial as you decide how much time to spend in your quiet corner and when. Don't cut yourself off from the world. If you feel cut off, perhaps you could spend some time redressing that. Use your time alone to create imaginative solutions to your isolation. Once you do, the character of your alone time will change. Your loneliness will diminish, and you will begin to value your time alone as never before. You will use your time more productively, and you will cross that thin line into harmony.

Procrastination

The effort that many of us put into not doing something or the time we spend thinking about doing something can be extremely stressful and anxiety producing. If you procrastinate, you probably worry about all the time you're wasting as you think about getting started. You probably don't waste as much time as you think you do, but this tendency to worry can make anyone feel harried and rushed. Our society has developed such a fevered pitch in relation to time that busyness is the expected mode of behavior. Time should not be wasted—after all, there's precious little of it. While this attitude can drive us into a whirlwind of doing, doing, doing, we sometimes are caught on the treadmill, rushing to nowhere.

If you find yourself worrying about the time you're wasting, or if you feel as if you're rushing and yet not actually doing anything, take a moment to breathe and consider your position. Are you actually procrastinating or are you simply mulling over your approach? A certain amount of mulling is necessary before settling down and doing a project. Observe your patterns and decide how much of your thinking time is wasted and how much of it is necessary and constructive. Then do the things you have to do and use some of your quiet-corner time as mulling time.

As you take some steps toward finding a quiet corner, you may feel some guilt pangs. The voices in your head may tell you that you could be doing something with this time. Why not use this time, since you've found it, in a constructive way? Why waste it on being quiet? Indeed, if you're an extremely busy, goal-oriented person—aren't we all, to some extent?—you will probably encounter this resistance each time you visit your corner. Even after your search begins, some time has passed, and you're practiced in the art of being in your quiet corner, you may continue to imagine that you're wasting time. Don't let this interference win out. Keep in mind that we're all conditioned to think this way and only diligence and time will change this pattern. As you begin to experience the enormous rewards of your quiet corner, collect them, and refresh your mind with these memories each time you encounter the waste-of-time bogeyman.

Spending/Saving Time

We are a culture obsessed with time—how much we have or how little we have. We are also under the illusion that we have time to spend or save as we choose. But as the saying goes, time waits for no one. Time just is. It is there whether we are or not and whether or not we pay attention to it.

When you first contemplate the idea of a quiet corner, pay no heed to the notion that you have no time to spend there. And once you free up some space in your busy life for this venture, try not to be influenced by the notion that reserving time is enough. This time will simply disappear if not used. You must continue to find the time each time. While at first it will seem like a Herculean effort, once you begin this process you will notice that time is not what you are manipulating. It is not an outer force that you must control. With time, you will notice that it is your attitude toward time, rather than time itself, that you have been adjusting all along.

And once you admit that you might have such an attitude toward time and that it might be interfering with your growth, you will be able to see how this attitude carries over into many areas of your life and colors your particular perspective on things. How you define events and new experiences will determine whether you see them as roadblocks or opportunities. Ask yourself what a silent retreat means to you. Do you immediately balk at the idea and imagine a time of solitary confinement? Or do you see it as an opportunity to explore your inner self? What about fasting? Is this just another word for starving yourself, or is it a means of purifying your body? Continue to question your attitudes, and work first on your attitude toward time. Once you adjust this and begin to spend some time in your quiet corner, you can use that time to reflect on some of your other attitudes and how they might be holding you back.

Quintessential Time

Scan your memory bank. What sorts of experiences are stored there? More than likely, you've probably retained those life events that are significant to you in some way. Your normal day-to-day life experiences probably don't qualify for safekeeping. Perhaps you have certain special accomplishments and achievements stored away—graduations and awards ceremonies, competitive sports events. And that overseas trip you took with your special friend or your summer camp buddy may be locked away in your heart and mind. No doubt there's some trauma and tragedy mixed in as well—a broken heart, the death of a loved one. While some of these memories may be painful to contemplate, each one changed your life in some way and carries with it a lesson about you and your world.

The time you spend in your quiet corner is likely to become significant enough that you will remember much of it years from now as time well spent. As you learn how to use this time, you will discover valuable information about yourself that will serve you in your everyday life. You will see yourself—the good and the bad—as never before, and you'll learn significant, memorable lessons that will qualify for your memory bank. You might also clean house a little bit, make peace with the memories that haunt you, and get rid of those that have served their purpose. A little quiet-corner time spent each day guarantees something worth remembering.

More about Breathing

As the days pass, you will have begun to practice your breathing and homed in on a quiet corner or two. You can now begin to extend your breathing practice. Once you settle into your corner, sit down in a comfortable, relaxed position. You can sit on cushions on the floor or sit upright in a chair. The important thing is to have your spine erect so that your breath will flow freely, naturally, and comfortably. Whether you choose the floor or a chair, it is a good idea to prop a small cushion under your buttocks so that you almost feel as though you're tilting forward. This will straighten your spine, and as you get used to this position, it will feel more comfortable than normal sitting.

When you're relaxed and comfortable, begin to concentrate on your breathing. As before, breathe slowly and deeply. Count each exhalation until you count ten breaths. Then begin again and count to ten. Continue—and continue. If it makes it easier to stay with the count, count each inhalation and each exhalation up to ten and then begin again. Each time you enter your quiet corner and practice this breathing exercise, lengthen the time you spend doing it. If you lose track of your count, simply return to one and begin again. If you find that your mind drifts and you are way beyond ten, simply stop and begin again. Your mind will not want to cooperate at first. But as you practice, your mind will quit resisting and settle down into the breath. You will gain immediate rewards from this practice. If you can sit and practice this breathing for ten, twenty, or thirty minutes, the rewards will multiply. You will achieve a calm that you never thought possible. The noise in your head, which was loud and overwhelming at first, will subside. You will leave your quiet corner a quieter person.

Facing Your Quiet Corner

Chances are that once you contemplate the idea of spending time quietly alone, you will feel some anxiety. It's perfectly normal, if you're accustomed to a fast-paced and constantly moving world, to become disoriented when the movement stops. Even the thought of jumping out of the rat race can raise some fears. Our mind can be our own worst enemy.

The antidote for this is slow, deep breathing. Conscious breathing is an instant, magical cure and instills in us the courage to move forward. Its power to transform us and lessen our fear should convince us to never take anything for granted.

When anxiety takes hold of you as you contemplate facing your quiet corner, simply resort to concentrated breathing and you will be able to take your next step. Breathe, breathe, and breathe some more.

Resistance

The garbage needs to be emptied. The cat's claws need to be clipped. The back closet needs cleaning, and that letter to Aunt Flo simply can't wait any longer. As you approach or think about entering your quiet corner, you may be distracted by the need to do something else. Don't be surprised by this. There are many diversions waiting for you that often look more inviting than your corner. This is your mind resisting the idea of quieting down and facing yourself.

Your fears feed your imagination, and your quiet corner suddenly looms large, loud, and threatening. Anything but facing your corner and yourself becomes attractive. The longer you resist entering your quiet corner, the more powerful the force not to becomes. All it takes is a step over that line of resistance. Once you commit yourself, make the decision, and then take that step, quiet ensues almost at once. You begin to wonder what all the noise was about. You relax and soon find yourself comfortable and peaceful in your quiet corner.

This resistance to enter your quiet corner may never disappear completely. You may meet it each time. Sometimes it may fool you and appear as a legitimate distraction. Keep your resolve and try not to be swayed. Simply acknowledge the resistance, accept it for what it is, and push through it into your quiet space, leaving it behind.

Energy

Finding the time, dealing with avoidance and fear, pushing through the resistance, learning to breathe again—you might be asking yourself, why bother? It all sounds like so much effort. Where will the energy come from, and is it worth it?

This is the Catch-22 of putting a quiet corner in your life. In order to get there, you do have to expend some energy. You get more back than you spend, but then you have to spend it for your next quiet corner. And so on and so on.

But as you continue the practice of your quiet corner, the quality of your energy will change and you will always have the energy you need. When you carry over your quiet-corner practices—breathing, mindfulness, and so forth—into other areas of your life, your energy will be constant and strong. You will rarely run out, and any loss of sleep you experience as a result of your quiet corner will more than be made up for in the energy you have gained. In order to get energy, you must spend a little, and once a quiet-corner practice becomes a cornerstone in your life, you will not recall how you once struggled to find the energy to get there. In fact, you will someday get to the point where you will retreat to your quiet corner in order to replenish your energy reserves.

The Paradox—So Easy, Yet So Hard

You need no special skills to face a quiet corner—no special talents, no special brainpower. Each one of us has the raw material necessary. Desire is a requirement, but if you're reading this, you already have that. Simply set some time aside, choose a spot, get comfortable, breathe, and voilà—a quiet corner! Sounds easy, so why is it so hard?

Fear of the unknown, of ourselves, of change. The idea of being quiet and alone with ourselves is a foreign one. Many of us are more comfortable in situations where we know what to expect, even if it's painful, than in situations where there's uncertainty. But life is uncertain, and even if we think we know how something will turn out, we don't.

If you push through the fear and concentrate on the easy aspects of your quiet corner, once you're in there you'll be able to deal with the hard aspects. If you don't take the risk, you'll never know. But if you do, once you're on the other side of your fear, you will be able to look at and understand it. Use the fear as your teacher, and the lessons you learn will be useful and everlasting. You may find that after a quiet-corner session, your fear has abated and your willingness to embrace change is strong. As a matter of fact, strength to face many areas of your life might surface, as facing your fear will give you courage to move into other previously scary territory. So dance with your fear, and glide into new and exciting arenas of personal exploration.

Who's Looking?

Awards ceremonies, diplomas, honor rolls, first-place medals, promotions, pay raises, scholarships—these are just some of the ways that our society recognizes and rewards achievement. It is often what motivates us, the carrot at the end of the stick. When we search for a quiet corner, there is no tangible carrot awaiting us. And we're not being graded. No one is watching.

We enter the stream alone and report back only to ourselves. The rewards are quiet, subtle ones—no marching bands. When we keep at it, those we love will share in the benefits without perhaps even knowing how or why. And there's no need to share the specifics of your transformation with others. Let it be your secret. Let your quiet corner be a place where you commune with yourself and, if it works for you, with your higher power. No one is watching. But everyone gains.

Acceptance

Through each step of the process of finding, facing, and using a quiet corner, you will learn a great deal about yourself. The first thing you might learn is how you deal with the process. While there is some instant gratification in three-part, three-breath breathing, most of the lasting and strengthening rewards of spending time in a quiet corner are gradual and subtle. An acceptance of this process will be necessary in order to enjoy the long-term benefits.

Your individual approach and your idiosyncrasies will become apparent throughout the process. Remember that there is no right way to do this. Accept your way. If you circle your corner in procrastination before finally entering, accept this as your process. If you dip in and out before settling down, accept this as your process. Whatever your approach is, if it works for you, it's the right way.

Some of what you learn may not sit well, and you may practice denial as you struggle toward perfection. But we are in process here, not perfection. Many Native American works of art contain intentional flaws because of the belief that only the Creator can create perfection. Keep this in mind as you sit in the process. And practice acceptance.

Projection

The anticipation of an event is often more thrilling than the event itself. This knack that we all seem to have, of projecting, fantasizing, and distorting reality, may sometimes serve us well. But it can also be our undoing. The idea of spending time alone may elicit feelings of both fear and pleasure. We may look forward to time alone as a welcome and refreshing reprieve from our hectic lives. But if we take this thought one step further, we may feel some dread about this unstructured time alone, fearing that we won't know what to do. And this might just keep us from facing our quiet corner.

The simple answer here is this: Just don't think ahead. While this may sound impossible, it's not. While it may not be easy, it is simple. Go ahead and reserve your quiet-corner time; then relax and don't think about it again until you're in it. Trust yourself. You'll know what to do. Keep the pleasure and the terror at bay. Simply plan to be in your quiet corner without attaching emotion to the experience before the experience begins.

As you move along your quiet-corner path and learn not to project about your time spent there, you can transfer this new skill to other areas of your life. Plan your next vacation, but try not to predict exactly how you'll spend your days or how you'll feel at the end of the trip. Simply make your plans and show up for the magic. Do likewise with other social and work events. Show up prepared, but be ready for anything. If you can do this, you will avoid disappointment and you will be open and available to the wonder of life and its magnificent treats and surprises. As you perfect this skill, you will see how your previous behavior was limiting you and how this new behavior opens your world to an abundance of possibilities. While this is all very exciting, remember not to get excited until the excitement is upon you. Then it will be truly glorious and real.

Faith

Even if you take all the suggestions in this book, you are bound to come up against a wall now and then. You may sometimes wonder exactly what you are doing, as nothing seems to be happening. And at times throughout this quiet-corner process (there's that term again!), you may question everything. At such times, you will need to reach into your heart and grab hold of some faith—faith that the process works, faith that you are on the right path, faith that all is not for naught.

Turning to faith to get you through the rocky moments will be especially critical as you begin this process. Further along the path, as you build up your experiences, you will be able to identify these illusionary roadblocks for what they usually are—annoying distractions that have no basis in reality. But in the beginning, faith is often necessary to push you through. And faith will come in handy as you continue your journey when all that you believed is called into question. Turning to faith early on in the process makes it much more accessible later on.

The word *faith* has been so closely associated with religion over the years that in some circles it has a negative connotation. If you are included in one of those circles, try for a moment to disassociate faith from religion. Think of faith as a heart thing that has nothing to do with your brain. Try to let go of the old meaning and don't attach any new meaning to it. Just try to feel it. First, challenge yourself and have faith in your ability to follow the quiet-corner path. From there, it's easy to transfer that faith to the process and know that as long as you proceed faithfully, you will be in sync with the process and the process will not fail you. Keep faith in your heart and you won't even have to think about it.

Let Your Breathing Guide You

Listen to your breath all along the way. As you proceed with finding a quiet corner, each time you settle into one, allow your breath, not your brain, to guide you. As thoughts rise, identify and accept them as thoughts and let them float away. Just breathe. As you breathe and concentrate on each breath, become aware of the source of your breath.

Lie on your back on the floor with your arms gently relaxed at your sides, palms up. Relax and breathe into your lower abdomen. As you inhale, notice your stomach rise. As you exhale, notice it fall. If your breath is stuck in your throat or chest, try sending it down to your abdomen. Place one palm on your stomach so that you can feel the motion of your breathing. If you've ever watched a young baby breathe, you will know how smooth, natural, and unhindered breathing can be. Try to breathe like a child. Each time you practice your breathing, come back to this exercise until this way of breathing becomes natural again in any position.

While it may take some time and practice to soften and deepen your breathing, turn to it at any point and use it as your guide. If your mind is clouded with too many thoughts and your brain is in overdrive, turn it all over to your breath and allow this natural rhythm to sort it all out. Take yourself out of the picture. Just breathe. If you are in your quiet corner and don't know what to do, listen to your breath and stop trying to make a decision. Let your breath do it for you. Give up that responsibility. Just breathe.

Quiet-Corner Walking

Do you jump in your car to go two blocks to the corner grocer? Do you hop on a bus to travel a mile to the movies? Do you drive to the train station in the morning rather than walk the half mile? If so, these are perfect opportunities to grab some quiet time and get some physical exercise as well.

Give yourself a little extra time and set out walking to your destination. Choose a posture and pace that feel comfortable and that suit your body. Begin walking slowly, inhaling and exhaling deeply as you do. Concentrate on your breathing as you walk. As your concentration deepens, you will become keenly aware of, but not distracted by, your surroundings. By softly focusing your eyes about three feet in front of you, your concentration will improve.

Try this walking exercise once or twice, and observe your state of mind when you reach your destination. I find that I'm relaxed and yet alert at the same time. Colors are deeper, images are sharper, and sounds are crisper. I have more patience in the slow-moving bank or grocery line.

There are many occasions during the day to practice quiet walking. Walk the stairs at work rather than take the elevator; practice a version of quiet walking as you walk the dog. Use your imagination, and remember to breathe.

Is This Meditation?

The dictionary offers a simple definition of *meditation*, but our minds tend to embellish the definition and make it into something mysterious and esoteric. There are many different types of meditation, and the external form of any one of them may be the image we carry in our minds of what meditation is. This image may scare us off from even contemplating meditation. Some people use words to meditate, some use images, and some use sounds. Many people also meditate with closed eyes, but I find that this can cause drowsiness and encourage daydreaming. For our purposes, let's define our quiet-corner practice simply as "concentrated breathing with eyes gently open." This is simple and effective.

As you begin to sit quietly in this fashion, breathing deeply, you may want to introduce an image or a sound into your practice to deepen your concentration, but this is not necessary. If all you ever do in your quiet corner is sit quietly with eyes open and breathe, you can consider yourself meditating.

Light a Candle

Since you will be sitting in your quiet corner breathing deeply with your eyes gently open, you might want to observe the source of light in your corner. If you find yourself there in the morning and your windows are enough to allow in natural light, open your shades wide and notice how the light changes as time passes. If you're there in the middle of the day, you might want to draw the shades to dim the light. At this time, you can also observe shifts in the light patterns. Drawing the shades is a way to soften the mood in the room and create an atmosphere that is unique to that time of day.

If your quiet time falls after the sun sets, light a candle, or light many candles. Candlelight can be especially soothing and create a special mood. There's something about the flickering light and the color generated that softens and changes your everyday surroundings. This will alter your perspective. And this is the true reason you need quiet-corner time. By lighting candles at the beginning of your quiet-corner period, you will be marking off this time as special. As you sit quietly in your corner filled with candle-light, cherish each moment and consider it perfect.

Burn Some Incense

The smell of cotton candy brings to mind amusement parks and the thrill of being a child. The smell of wet, fallen leaves brings the sad memory of summer's end and the happy one for some of us of school's beginning. For most of us, our sense of smell is rather strong and peculiar to our individual tastes and personalities. Unpleasant smells may dampen our mood, while pleasant ones bolster it.

When I set aside time to spend in my corner, I first light some incense. The smell signifies to me that my quiet time has begun. I'm less likely to allow distractions. I determine how much incense will burn in the time I've allotted myself, freeing me to concentrate on my quiet-corner activity without consulting my watch. I make a ritual of lighting incense every time I visit my corner, and the smell of it has an immediate calming effect. Each time I smell incense, I am reminded of my quiet corner. This smell has been added to the others in my sense memory, and it always invokes quietude.

Buy an incense burner or simply burn your incense in a favorite cup or small bowl. When you begin, you will need some pebbles or some salt to stand the incense upright. As ashes accumulate, use them to stick the incense into, and after each session in your quiet corner, smooth out the ashes so that they're neat and ready for your next visit.

Beginning and ending my quiet-corner time with the incense ritual gives a frame to that time and gives me an activity that expresses my commitment to spending time with myself.

Entertain Yourself

We are constantly being barraged with entertainment—the music in restaurants, the video images in many stores, highway billboards, computer games and networks, TV talk shows, TV nightly news and magazine shows, late-night TV shows, movies, videotapes, video games, magazines, and web sites. The list is endless. All of these forms of entertainment compete for our time. And there's never enough time to do it and see it all, despite the pressure put on us to do so. Small wonder why so many of us crave some quiet time but aren't quite sure how to use it.

The first step is to lessen the amount of outside stimulation that enters your world. You do have some control over this. Think carefully about what you allow into your life. Before you turn on the radio or TV, make a conscious decision about it. Think about what you want to hear and see, and proceed with that in mind. If you notice yourself mindlessly tuning in or half-listening to a program, or surfing the net aimlessly, spend that time in your quiet corner instead. Think of it as self-entertainment.

If you wake every morning to the sound of your favorite radio station blaring in your ear, you might consider using a gentler alarm and rising in silence. Wait at least a half hour before you tune in to the news and weather as you prepare for your day. If you read the paper every morning, perhaps taking a break from the printed news every other day would free up some quiet time. Try this for a week or two to determine how much important news you actually miss. If you turn the evening news on when you get home from work and leave the TV on as entertainment, you might try watching an hour less each day. Again, decide at the end of a week if you've missed anything worthwhile. If you check your e-mail first thing in the morning, try skipping that every other day. Slowly but surely, you will replace much of your leisure time with quiet-corner time and be stimulated in a way that can never be achieved by external stimulation.

Consult the Child in You

Some of my warmest childhood memories are of spending summer evenings on the back stoop with the neighborhood kids and all our mothers. We had our baths and were in our pajamas. We couldn't romp around too much because we were already cleaned up for bed, but we found many ways to have fun. And our clean bodies and cotton pj's made us feel safe and comforted with our mothers chatting in the background.

To achieve this feeling as an adult, I dress in baggy cotton sweatpants and oversized T-shirts. And as much as possible, I walk around barefoot, especially in my quiet corner.

So as to separate your quiet-corner time from the everyday, that is, until all of your time is quiet-corner time, look to your childhood and incorporate elements into your quiet corner that made you particularly happy back then. Or think of something that you always wanted as a child and incorporate that. Perhaps you might set up a fish tank in your quiet-corner space or paste stars on the ceiling of your room. Be creative, have fun, and remember to consult with the child in you whenever you make those quiet-corner decisions.

Read Quietly Aloud to Yourself

Enter your quiet corner and settle yourself down with some concentrated breathing. Select a favorite story or poem and slowly and carefully read it out loud. You may want to start this exercise by reading aloud a favorite children's story. There's a wealth of material to choose from. If reading out loud at first seems awkward to you, you can pretend to be reading to a child. Or you can read to yourself as if you were the child and either relive the experience of being read to or experience the pleasure for the first time. You could also read passages from this book, especially the ones on breathing, to remind yourself to breathe. One of the benefits of reading aloud is that, in order to do it, you must breathe, and as you proceed, your breathing will become deeper and smoother.

If you want to share your quiet-corner time with another person, you could take turns reading to each other. Beginning and ending this time with a shared period of silence could lend a feeling of sacredness to the time. It would also introduce you to the power of sitting in silence with another breathing human being—one who shares your interest in this process.

Try to breathe from your abdomen as you read aloud. Take the words from deep within you, and let your breath carry them forward and out into the world.

Practice, Practice, Practice

Whatever gain you get from your quiet corner today may carry through to tomorrow, but it will begin to fade if you don't continue the practice of taking quiet-corner time. And while the effects of this practice are cumulative, you must practice daily in order for this to be so. As with anything worthwhile, your quiet-corner experience gets better with practice and time.

There will be many days when retreating to your quiet corner will seem to take more effort than you think it's worth. Go there anyway. There may be days when you feel stuck and your quiet corner seems more like a burden than a luxury. Go there anyway. Even if you feel you can spare only ten minutes some days, that's enough. If you wait for the perfect time, the perfect motivation, and the perfect setting, you may never get there. Keep going there and practice your practice.

Make It a Habit

If you're like most people, you probably have a set way of doing most things, whether it's what you eat for breakfast or how you wash your body during your shower. More than likely, you have established certain habitual ways of doing things that you rarely even notice or give much thought to. While the breathing practices, the search for quiet corners, and the mindful approach to life suggested in this book are all meant to break these habitual patterns and allow you to see your world from a different angle, your tendency to establish habits can serve you well as you begin this journey.

Decide that putting a quiet corner in your day is as crucial to your survival and well-being as your daily shower or evening meal. Force yourself to include time for yourself every day until quiet-corner time becomes a habit and your equilibrium gets thrown off if you miss a day. Once this time becomes a necessary part of your life, you can use it to review all your habitual patterns and break them down one by one. Making your quiet corner a habit will help you to see and perhaps change all your other habits.

Cultivate Your Own Distinct Style

There is no absolute right way to do any of this. Everything here is but a suggestion, an outline for you to use as you proceed along your unique path toward self-awareness. The intention for each of us in this process is to wake up the spirit. And just as we all have a different internal clock, we also all have different sensibilities. Our individual moods are wont to change, and the perfect approach today might be a disaster tomorrow. So take from this book what works for you and leave the rest. Build on this structure to construct your own quiet-corner system.

As you create your quiet corner, and spend more time there, your self-awareness will heighten. Your likes and dislikes will become more apparent, yet you won't judge yourself. You'll simply begin to accept the various elements—good and bad—that make you who you are. Use this knowledge as you cultivate your quiet-corner experiences. It is in your quiet corner that you can experiment with new aspects of yourself and bury old ones that no longer work for you. Don't be afraid to entertain the suggestions of others, but don't lock yourself into someone else's vision. Spread your wings in your quiet corner so that you will fly into the world with your personal style in full feather.

Ritual

Doing the same thing over and over in the same way and manner can often lead to bewilderment. For instance, if we perform the same tasks every morning as we prepare for our day and follow the same route to our destination, we might zone out and forget whether we actually mailed those bills and letters we thought we were carrying when we left the house. Or if we sit in front of the TV or computer every night, we might wonder at week's end where the time went and feel dull and listless. This may be confused with ritual, but it is just our habitual patterns at work.

Ritual is something else entirely and can be invigorating and liberating. Ceremonial ritual can imbue life with order and purpose. When we observe certain rituals being performed, whether in the secular or the religious world, we may not always understand the meaning, but we can probably appreciate the beauty. If we bring some of this ritual into our quiet corner, we can mark this time as special. Lighting candles or incense, reading the same passage each time, beginning and ending the time with a favorite prayer or song—even these small touches after a while will carry great significance. And if we ritualize our quiet-corner time, we will find freedom within the ritual to move beyond the ordinary and begin to gain a new understanding and appreciation of our world. Continuing this practice beyond your quiet corner and introducing ritual into all your activities will make even a mundane chore such as washing the dishes a remarkable event.

Keep It Yours

No two minds work alike, no two bodies react the same way, and no one else has your individual stamp, so try not to compare your experiences and progress in your quiet corner with anyone else's. Since we seem to attract people with similar interests, some of your friends and family members may also be on the quiet-corner path. It is often necessary and helpful to compare notes and to share experiences, but be careful to avoid thinking that others are doing everything right and you are doing it wrong, or vice versa. That is impossible. You have your style, they have theirs, and both styles are perfect.

Also, while it is helpful and advisable to take suggestions from others who have been on the path longer, it is not necessary to force yourself into something that doesn't fit. At the same time, keep in mind that all of this will seem awkward and uncomfortable at first, so try to avoid using this awkwardness as an excuse not to change. Discomfort is different from twisting yourself into someone else's pattern. You will quickly be able to discern the difference. You will know what is right for you. You will learn to accept your way and respect the ways of others. Your way is not the only way, but it is yours.

Sharing

If you have friends or family members who are also committed to finding a quiet corner, you may want to start a quiet corner group. This shared experience is unlike any other and will teach you much about the world and your place in it. The group experience will also help you if you are having trouble with self-discipline.

You might want to begin each group session with a prayer, song, or chant that you all recite together out loud. Or you might want each person to light a candle or a stick of incense before you begin. Or you might choose to have one person each time share an individual quiet-corner experience that you all can concentrate on. Perhaps the members could take turns orchestrating a session. Or you could all agree beforehand how the session should evolve. Try to keep it simple, though.

Most important, be sure that some of this quiet corner time is just that, quiet. Decide to spend a certain amount of this time sitting in complete silence. You could arrange for a small bell to ring signifying the beginning and end of this silent period so that no one will have to watch the clock and everyone will feel free to let go. With two or more people sitting together in silence, breathing and concentrating, amazing things will begin to happen. Extend the silent period each time you meet as a group. First try ten minutes, then twenty, and so on. The longer you sit together in shared silence, the greater the rewards. Sharing in this way will put you in touch with each other as nothing else will, and this experience could alter your view of the universe.

Prayer

When you step into your quiet corner, you might want to formally acknowledge that there is a force at work in the world that you have no control over. Whether you believe this force to be God or physics or nature or your higher self, it doesn't matter. If you've given this some thought, you will probably agree that there is something bigger and more powerful than you in the universe, even if you don't have a name for it. One way to invite this force into your world is with prayer. And beginning and ending your quiet-corner time with prayer frames that time with reverence.

A prayer can be viewed simply as an invocation to a force outside yourself or deep within you that will unlock your heart and open it to a fresh outlook. These invocations, inspirational sayings, or prayers can be found in many places. The many and varied religions and cultures of the world and our greatest thinkers and spiritual leaders have provided a plethora of prayers for you to choose from. A trip to your local bookstore will immediately reveal the rich source of inspiration available to you. As you make your selections, you might want to read a different prayer each time you visit your quiet corner. As you discover new prayers, there may be one or two that you commit to memory so that you can use them during the day when you find yourself in a jam or when you feel tense. Silently reciting a prayer over and over often relieves tension and will help guide you through the rough spots.

The beauty of the language in most prayers is often enough to wake me up and alter my perspective. I begin to view the world in a new light and become ready for any challenge. My quiet-corner experience is profoundly moving when prayer is a part of it.

Insomnia

Tossing and turning all night, thoughts of what didn't get done today and what must get done tomorrow, misery over the breakup of a relationship, grief over the death of someone dear, worry about a sibling or child, too many bills to pay, and on and on.

No one is exempt from troubles, and we've all had our share of sleepless nights. But instead of lying in torment, consider this an opportunity to retreat to a quiet corner. You won't be getting any sleep anyway, and the rest of your world is down for the night, so why not spend some extra time in your corner? You can face some of the demons that are squawking at you, and you'll be less tired in the morning for your efforts.

When you reach your quiet corner, keep the lights down low or use candles. Sit on some cushions on the floor and be sure you're warm enough. Make your corner cozy and comfortable. Now breathe. As each disturbing or obsessive thought rises, breathe. Continue breathing deeply with your eyes gently open. See the fear attached to the worry. Breathe. Notice your own attachment to that person. Breathe. Yesterday is over, tomorrow not yet here. Breathe. You are right now in a warm place, secure for the moment. Continue breathing as your thoughts slow down. Perhaps some insight will be yours as you proceed and breathe through your worry. You may soon find yourself nodding off, ready for sleep. Breathe a little more before returning to bed, and continue the practice as you lie down. Breathe yourself into a peaceful sleep.

When Things Don't Go Your Way

We all have days, weeks, or even longer periods when we feel stretched to our limit. The least little thing can set us off and cause us to behave in a manner that is unbecoming and perhaps unkind. At times like this, we might become inflexible, setting rigid standards for, and expectations of, ourselves and others. Normally, if our train is late or if our child or pet gets sick, we would take it in our stride. But there are times when it seems as if the world is actually against us, as if circumstances are conspiring to aggravate us, and nothing seems to be going our way. These are especially important times to spend a few moments taking stock.

You might be aware of your behavior and feel there is nothing you can do about it. You shrug it off and decide that it will pass at some point. But there's no need to wait until it passes. Sitting in the negative energy of such times only hurts you and those around you.

One very simple exercise you can do, even though it's the last thing you might think of doing, is smile. If your facial muscles won't cooperate because your frown is winning the fight, simply force your mouth into a smile with your fingers. Even this will begin to change your mood. Breathe as you do this, and allow yourself to feel silly. Continue to push your face into a smile until you feel yourself relaxing and the tension easing. At some point, you may even be able to laugh out loud at yourself and your struggle to make everything work the way you want it to work, when you want it to work. The world just doesn't always cooperate. And there is humor in this if you give yourself a moment to see it. So smile when you least expect to and your expectations won't get the best of you.

Turn Bad Situations to Your Advantage

"Take some time along the way to stop and smell the roses." While this suggestion may appear dated and old-fashioned, it seems that collectively we've moved so far from this that the goal has become all important and the route is but a nuisance. We focus on the outcome or intention of each event, even a simple chore or outing. Everyday activities are conducted on automatic pilot so that much of our day is a blur.

When your path seems littered with obstructions and you become impatient and irritable, take a moment and consider just why you are annoyed. Are you at your destination before you even arrive? The next time you are sitting in traffic, on your way to some other place, take note of your reactions. Are you disturbed because you'll be late or because such situations make you feel totally helpless? Reflect on the why and how of your feelings. This is a terrific opportunity to take a moment to become more familiar with yourself. It's also a perfect time to create a quiet corner. You can't go anywhere, the situation is completely out of your control, and this is private time you might not otherwise have found. Breathe deeply and calm down. Enjoy the gift rather than cursing the misfortune.

Have you ever actually timed the traffic light that won't turn green quickly enough? Next time you're sitting there drumming the steering wheel, breathe deeply a few times and actually time the light. It will seem to change much sooner if you are calm and relaxed than if you are rushed and anxious. Take advantage of the time-out.

And as you stand in the slow-moving ticket line, talk to

your neighbor about the show you are about to see rather than the poor management of the theater. Or, again, spend this time standing calmly in your quiet corner, and breathe. Your enjoyment of the show and of your day will be greatly enhanced.

Breathe

As you spend more and more time in your quiet corner, and as your concentration improves, you might begin to notice a few things. First, while the cessation of thought might be your ultimate desire, you won't stop thinking. But you will have more and longer periods with little mind interference. These moments of quiet will prepare you for the onslaught of thoughts that is sure to come. When it does come, try to use your new powers of concentration and fortitude to simply notice these thoughts as thoughts, and then let them go. Try not to latch on to a thought or to continue thinking the thought. Acknowledge that you are having a thought, breathe, and wait for the next one. Don't follow any one thought.

As you sit concentrating on your breathing, detaching yourself from your thoughts, you will become aware of your breath in a surprising and unusual way. You can get to the point where you will notice that your breath is breathing you. You are not actually breathing; your breath is breathing. This is a strangely liberating experience and one that's hard to imagine as you read this. But if you continue your breathing, thinking and not thinking, and let your breath breathe you, the experience will be yours.

Singing

Have you ever wondered why most religious ceremonies include songs or chants? Even sports events—a religion to many—begin with the national anthem. Singing is a magnificent form of expression, and it has the benefit of being a physically healthful exercise, as well.

Once you've settled yourself into your corner by sitting quietly and consciously breathing, slowly begin to chant or sing some passages that you've selected beforehand. Choosing something unfamiliar will force you to concentrate that much harder on each syllable, and this will force other distracting thoughts from your mind, freeing you to concentrate even more. As you sing, become aware of your breathing. Bring each sound up from your abdomen along with your breath. Keeping your spine erect will allow your breath and each sound to flow smoothly.

Experiment with the tempo and volume. For instance, you might want to start off slowly and quietly and build up to fast and loud. Once you stop, sit in silence for a few moments and bask in the stillness. You will probably be more sensitive to the sounds around you: The birds outside your window may sound especially musical and cheerful; the rain on your windows might sound friendly and warm. You might even discover some new sounds around you. Continue breathing. You will find a difference in your breathing practice after singing or chanting. Your diaphragm and your heart will be more open than usual, allowing your silent breathing to work its miracle in your quiet corner.

Calming the Mind

Concentrated breathing, silent sitting, chanting, and singing—all of these are simply techniques to quiet the chatter in our brains so that we can observe our true and natural selves. With so many external stimuli and so much overstimulation in our lives, it's not easy to find the quiet. There may be quiet-corner sessions where you never actually find the quiet. Don't be discouraged. The quiet will come.

And the quiet will bring calmness of mind. And a calm mind will bring calmness of spirit. Within this calm, you will be able to look with some detachment at your thoughts and your behavior. Your place in the world will become clearer, and confusion will diminish. Answers to vexing problems will become apparent. It is simple but not easy. Just sit still and breathe quietly, and a calm mind will be yours.

Where Is the Mind and Who Is Its Master?

As you spend more and more time in your quiet corner, breathing and noticing your thoughts, devote a few sessions to concentrating on the source of your thoughts. Where are they coming from? What generates them? Why this particular thought in this particular moment and not another? Be the observer as your mind works.

Distancing yourself from the workings of your mind and the thoughts that arise will enable you to gain some perspective on yourself. Just slowing down and listening to your own internal rhythm will make a difference. Even the simple willingness to do this will have a profound impact on your life.

Your mind may often seem to have a mind of its own. No matter how much you bid it to slow down and be quiet, if it wants to be busy and noisy it will be. As you sit and listen to this noise, ask yourself why it exists. What, other than you, is driving it? The answer may not be readily apparent, now or ever. But in order to gain some serenity in this world, it is important to ask the question.

Concentration

Concentrated fruit juice is essentially juice with all the water, a nonessential ingredient, drained out of it. You would not want to drink juice in this pure form, however. Before you can drink it, that nonessential ingredient, water, must be put back in.

Think of meditation and time spent in your quiet corner as a means of removing the nonessential ingredients from your life for a short time. As with the juice, you will at some point discover that nothing is nonessential, but spending some time in concentration is one way to discover this.

There are many different concentration techniques. Experiment with different ones and use the ones that work for you. You might repeat one word over and over in your mind, concentrating on the form, shape, and meaning of that word. Choose a word that means nothing to you; a foreign word might work best. Or focus on an image. Visualize something in your mind, or place an object in front of you. Devote all your attention to this image or object. And don't forget to breathe. Breathing, of course, is another way to concentrate. Count your breaths; simply follow your breath and set your mind fully on it. If you can't concentrate on both the inhalation and the exhalation, concentrate on just a half breath, or simply let your breath breathe, and pay attention. Repeating a phrase over and over in your mind is also a good way to concentrate. Choosing one that brings your attention to the current moment may be most effective.

As your ability to concentrate improves, elements of your

life that you once regarded as nonessential and perhaps bothersome will either fade away or become integrated. You will be calmer and much more capable of accepting the previously unacceptable. The how and why of this process will more than likely remain a mystery. So be it.

Love

You may be asking yourself, what does all this have to do with love? How does love fit in with a quiet corner? If I take myself away from the world every day and sit in a quiet corner by myself, am I not taking time away from others with whom I want to spend time and to whom I want to express love? These are all valid questions, and if you're asking them, you're probably ready to hear the answers.

If you are committed to the quiet-corner path, every part of your being and every aspect of your life will be affected. The changes will at first seem to be subtle, minor changes. But as time passes, you will learn to accept how profound each one really is. Your quiet-corner practice of concentration will increase your awareness, and that in turn will introduce more patience and tolerance into your life. These will determine first how you treat yourself and then how you treat others. As you grow, your ability to feel and express compassion will also grow. As you come to understand yourself and the motives behind your behavior, you will appreciate others more and have an increased capacity to practice unconditional love. Your expectations will not be what they once were, and there will be more room in your life for love as well as more time for it. Taking time out for your daily quiet corner will yield an abundance of love. So begin by loving yourself enough to find your quiet corner, and you will be rewarded with more than enough love. Understanding yourself and others is the key to love. Simply retreat to your quiet corner and breathe.

Progress, Not Perfection

If you're anything at all like me, you hate to settle for less than perfection. This attitude causes endless disappointment and much blaming and finger-pointing. The finger may often point back at you, and it carries enough negativity and judgment to do some serious damage. Let's nip this attitude in the bud before it has the opportunity.

If you gain nothing from this book but the understanding that life in all its aspects is ever-changing, unpredictable, and not controllable by any of us, that's enough. If you slowly but surely come to realize that you are perfect as you are, that's enough. If you decide to introduce some quiet corners into your life, with no expectations, that's enough.

While each one of us, and everything about our lives, are perfect just as they are, very few of us believe this. But if we believe that we are less than perfect, give up the struggle to be perfect, and concentrate on the process—that's perfection. In your quiet corner, you can get in touch with this perfection. Know that there you are perfect, that everything is perfect.

When you enter your quiet corner, leave your private personal judge outside. As you learn to do without this judge while in your corner, try to exclude it from other areas of your life, as well. Before you know it, this judge will be off your shoulder for good. And your progress on the quiet-corner path will be less hindered. Perfect.

Drawing and Writing

If you are visually oriented and tend to learn through seeing, drawing or painting could be one of your quiet-corner activities. If drawing is already a part of your life, change the way you draw in your quiet corner so that you might see differently. If you normally draw at a desk, try moving to the floor; if you prefer to draw on an easel, move to a table. If you don't now draw but would like to, experiment with different positions. Bookend each drawing session with silent sitting and concentrated breathing exercises. Use your quiet-corner drawing time to focus on whatever thoughts come to you when you sit and breathe. What thought keeps recurring? How does each thought look to you? Draw or paint it so that you can take a closer look. Are you sitting in a pool of anger? What does that look like? Where are you in the picture? As you record your thoughts and feelings, try not to edit what you draw. These drawings are for your eyes only. You might even consider destroying them after each session. That would mark a significant beginning in learning the discipline of detachment.

If you think in words rather than images and learn best from the written word, you might want to keep a quiet-corner journal. Designate a special notebook and pen to be used only in your quiet corner. Keep them in a safe and private place for you alone. At some point in this process, you may want to share parts of this journal with a trusted friend or adviser, but as you write, pretend that you will be the sole audience. It is much easier to be honest this way.

Each time you enter your quiet corner, sit in silence for a while and do some concentrated breathing exercises while observing your mind. Then write about your thoughts and feelings. Sit quietly again after each writing session so as to observe the difference. The act of writing will often free certain thoughts from your mind that once seemed trapped. It will deflate some feelings to a size that seems manageable. And it will teach you a great deal about yourself.

Freeing your thoughts and feelings through drawing or writing will increase your self-awareness and prepare you to be more observant and tolerant when you are not in your quiet corner.

What Is the Sound of One Hand Clapping?

This Zen question has been used and overused, understood and misunderstood, joked about and taken seriously. At first glance, it's a seemingly innocuous and ridiculous question. But it and other such questions can serve a purpose as you spend time in your quiet corner and develop your concentration techniques.

When I was a child, the concept of God and eternity both confounded and pleased me. My friends and I never tired of asking questions such as "If God has always been there, when did He first start and who created Him?" We could not wrap our young minds around the notion of beginning-less beginning and endless end. My mature mind doesn't have a firm grasp on this concept, either, but I feel less frustrated today than I did as a child when contemplating such matters.

Today, I love questions such as "If a tree falls in the forest and there's no one around to hear it, does it make any sound?" There may be no answer or many answers to this question; it doesn't matter. I delight in letting the question swim around in my brain. Contemplating such paradoxes takes my mind off my petty everyday troubles and forces me to concentrate.

These questions are excellent tools to use in your quiet corner to improve your concentration. Once you've established your quiet corner and spent some time there practicing your breathing, choose a question that at one time boggled your mind; sit quietly and try to think of nothing else. When you get to this stage in your practice, you might want to seek guidance from someone who has been asking such questions for a long time. But for now, just go to your quiet corner, breathe, and ask yourself, "What is the sound of one hand clapping?"

Who Are You? Where Did You Come From? Where Are You Going?

On the face of it, these seem to be very simple questions. And you probably answer them often, especially when introducing yourself to new people or when describing your lifestyle. But when you take these questions into your quiet corner and spend some time with them, contemplating their true meaning and all the possible answers, you will never again see yourself simply as a name, address, and profession, even if you continue to describe yourself in those terms.

Most of us have probably given some thought to what might happen to us after we die. Many of us may even have a firm belief about the afterlife. But how many have considered the question of what happened to us before we were born? If something happens to us after death, why not before birth? While there may be no easy answer and many possibilities, contemplating such a question can be worthwhile and will reveal much about your perspective on life.

So retreat to the solace of your quiet corner and, when ready, ask yourself who you really are when your name, personality, and labels are stripped away. Ask yourself where you might have come from other than your mother's womb. Think of your death and ask yourself where you will be then. If you have no answers to these questions, or if you have many answers, it's all the same, because you may come to some realizations about your life that will matter just by asking the questions. And meanwhile, the disagreement with your boss or the concern about your finances will take on a new texture. Your perception of your place in the world will change. And this is why we ask ourselves these seemingly unanswerable questions in the quiet of our quiet corner.

Relaxing

Lounging in the sun, luxuriating in a hot tub, curling up with a good novel, or fishing in an isolated stream—these are all legitimate and enjoyable ways to relax and recover from the stresses of our fast-paced lives. Most of us relax when we participate in leisure-time activities. However, the relaxation you can achieve from spending time in your quiet corner is different and cannot be compared with these traditional relaxing experiences.

In a quiet corner, there often exists some tension—tension from concentrating on your breath or on some frustrating question, tension from observing the thoughts and feelings that cause you discomfort, tension from sitting still and not moving for a short time, tension from confronting yourself and your shortcomings. Even as you read this, you might be thinking that picking up a good book and getting lost in the story seems preferable to creating such tension. And some days that is the perfect choice. But the rewards of quiet-corner tension are magnificent and certainly better than a sunburn.

There is a simple physical exercise you can do to help you appreciate the partnership of tension and relaxation. Lie on the floor flat on your back with your arms at your sides, palms up. Notice how your body feels against the floor. Where are the tense areas? Raise one leg off the floor, tense your muscles as hard as you can, hold that position, then release the tension, drop your leg back onto the floor, and forget about it. Raise and lower the other leg. Do the same with your arms, hips, torso, shoulders, and head. When you raise your head, squeeze your eyes closed and pucker up your face. Hold the tension for a few seconds before letting go. When you're finished, observe how your body now feels against the floor. Is your body less tense? More relaxed?

When you sit in your quiet corner with tension, you will slowly learn how tension manifests itself in your life, and how to ease that tension. The relaxation you will experience after an intense quiet-corner session will come in the form of joyous and heightened awareness. You will probably find yourself smiling more. Your mind will be calmer and more relaxed. And as time passes and you develop your particular quiet-corner style, you will bring your practice into other activities and learn to relax in all areas of your life.

Sound

Train whistles, church bells, birdsongs, ocean waves—these sounds are pleasing for most of us. Blaring car horns, jackhammers, loud music, street traffic—most of us consider these sounds very disturbing. And when we're irritable or expecting quiet, almost any environmental sound can displease us. So, while this whole book is about *quiet* corners, try not to take that word too literally. Of course, the quieter the better, but don't search for a space that is hermetically sealed and dead silent. In fact, having some extraneous sound enter your quiet corner could be a good thing.

While you're sitting in your quiet corner concentrating on your breath or on some question, your concentration may be interrupted by the sounds of traffic or your neighbors' kids. When this happens, concentrate on the noise instead of becoming irritated by it. Why does the sound disturb you? What can you do about it? What memories or feelings does it stimulate? Before long, you might notice that the noise has abated, or at least it is not as bothersome. You may come to accept such noise as part of your environment and allow it to go on without letting it disturb you. And this will carry over into the rest of your life, teaching you to accept what is happening around you without becoming irritated or trying to interfere.

If you are particularly sensitive to sound, as you sit in your quiet corner dealing with the unpleasant sounds, you may also notice some pleasing sounds that you never noticed or paid attention to before—the fire station whistle marking the hour or the quiet tick of a grandfather clock. If your mind is quiet, your surroundings will be quiet. And it is in your quiet corner that you can learn to quiet your mind.

Clutter

Clutter interferes with our spiritual progress. When we clutter up our day with endless projects, we have no time left for ourselves. When we allow our physical spaces to become crowded with things, we have to wade through the clutter and sit amid confusion. Notice how calm most museums are: They are simply about the art being shown; there is nothing extraneous.

It's a simple matter to clear away some of the clutter in our lives and avoid creating more. Begin in your designated quiet corner. Diligence in keeping all clutter out of this space will bring rewards. As you spend more time sitting in a clutter-free environment, notice its calming effect. How extraordinary it would be to carry this tranquility to all areas of our lives. As you go through your day, be mindful of your actions and take care not to create unnecessary clutter. It all begins with awareness, and our quiet corner can be our guide.

Beauty

Whether you have a private corner of your house in which to set up a permanent quiet corner or whether you need to transform your space each time you visit your quiet corner, you will want to have near you something of beauty. An uncluttered space that is visually pleasing with a touch of beauty will set a peaceful and calming mood. This needn't take a large investment, and you might even strive for simplicity. Bring one fresh flower each time and place it in the vase you chose especially for your quiet corner. Or place a large seashell near your candleholder and incense burner. Or hang a nature photograph near where you sit.

If you decide to use your quiet-corner time to draw or write, purchase a specially crafted drawing pad or notebook for yourself. You could even wrap it in a silk scarf and tuck it away in a drawer for safekeeping between visits. Include special paintbrushes and pens. Your quiet-corner ritual could involve unwrapping your notebook and carefully folding the scarf or draping it over a cushion, adding to the beauty of the setting.

The more time you spend in your quiet corner, the more you will notice the beauty around you. You will take great pleasure in arranging flowers, in setting the table. More than likely, you will begin to introduce small touches of beauty into all your personal spaces. Beauty can transform more than just the space. Experiment with it in your quiet corner and let your creativity take over.

Comfort versus Discomfort

Whether it is learned or innate, it does seem that we will go to any length to avoid pain. And we will pay almost any price for pleasure and comfort. The odd thing about this is that, if we're paying attention, we come to realize that pain is inevitable and part of the wonder of being human. And we may notice that our searching and grasping for comfort only causes more pain.

To help you understand the discomfort in your life and how you deal with it, you can do a simple exercise in your quiet corner. Choose a comfortable sitting position, cross-legged on the floor or upright in a chair, making sure that your spine is erect and your hands loose in your lap. Begin your breathing exercises, and commit yourself to not moving for at least ten minutes. You might want to scratch an itch or blow your nose—try not to. Just sit still. Your leg might fall asleep, or you might want to adjust your posture to ease the strain in your neck. Just sit still. While this may sound like unnecessary torment, if you do this exercise a few times, you will learn a great deal about pain and your resistance to it. When you feel some physical discomfort, breathe into that area and relax. Accept that you are in physical pain and will be for a few minutes.

After a few sessions like this, you may notice that the pain distracted you from other worries that now seem unimportant. You may also notice that when you focus on the pain or try to resist it, it intensifies, but if you are able to concentrate on your breathing and accept the pain, it will lessen and may even disappear completely. While you may not experience

this immediately, you will eventually. As you continue practicing this exercise, your approach and attitude toward other
types of discomfort in your life will change over time. You
will find that the less you resist, the greater will be your
comfort.

Detachment

Perhaps the most difficult quiet-corner concept to grasp is that of detachment. Yet it is the key to freedom and peace. The most important question you can ask yourself each time you recognize an attachment to something is "How important is it?"

We all form attachments—to people, places, and things. Fear is most likely the underlying force here—fear of not having enough, fear of being alone, fear of failure, and so on. And our attachments, while we think they are normal and warranted, cause us a great deal of pain. We tend to think that we have control over them. Only when we lose them, or as we struggle to hold on to them, do we learn that we never had them in the first place.

Your quiet corner is the perfect place to sit with yourself and review your attachments, what they mean to you and what it would mean to lose them. It is here that you can learn how to detach yourself from the people and things in your life, and to do it with love. And rather than taking you further from the ones you love and making you cold and distant (which is what I once thought detachment was all about), it will bring you closer to people and will teach you how to express love without asking for anything in return. Because you will no longer have an emotional investment in how other people behave, they will gain the freedom to express their love as they need to. And you will learn to love them as they are.

Detaching yourself from the things in your life does not mean doing without or discarding money and nice things. It simply means trying not to make the attainment of such things an end in itself and not allowing them to become all important and the focus of your life. Collect things around you if you must, but be ready to let go of them at any moment with no regrets. Detach from these things before you lose them, and having or not having them will be one and the same.

Focus on the Moment

The ultimate aim of quiet-corner practice is to bring ourselves into the present moment, to make ourselves aware of what is happening now—not yesterday or tomorrow, but now. It is to bring us into this moment and keep us here. You may not yet be aware that you are not always living in the moment. But as you continue on the quiet-corner path, your awareness will improve. You will notice more readily when you are regressing or projecting. When you do notice this happening, try centering your attention on your breath. Your breath will always help you focus on the present. If you take three deep breaths at such times, you will notice where you are and how you're feeling. Take stock of yourself. Look around you and notice something about your surroundings. Place yourself firmly in the present by taking note of the shoes you're wearing. Take three more deep breaths and notice your posture. Are you holding on to some tension? Breathe into it and let it go. What activity are you engaged in? Bring all your attention to it and breathe. Don't think about finishing it—just be in it.

Don't Just Do Something—Sit There

When someone offered this advice to me years ago, I thought I had misheard it. Being a person of action, I would always look for something to *do*, particularly when I was uncomfortable. I've since learned that rather than dealing with the issue at hand, I was running away. I now sit with my thoughts and feelings so as to better understand myself.

When you're feeling sad, lonely, angry, happy, jealous, and so forth, try not to immediately do something about it. Go to your quiet corner and sit down. Breathe your way to understanding. Observe all aspects of your feelings. Try to have compassion for the person who may have inspired the feeling. Write about it. Talk to someone else about it. Think it through.

Whenever you think there must be something more you can do, it may be time to retreat to your quiet corner and extend the time you normally spend there. Use what you've learned along your quiet-corner path and build on that. Light your incense, light your candle, sit quietly, and breathe. If you want to push yourself to do something, do it there. Sit for twenty silent minutes if you can. Regulate your breathing and don't force anything. Just sit. If thoughts come, let them come, and go. If feelings come, let them come, and go. If you experience physical pain, let it be, and let it go. This may be the most difficult thing you can do, because in a sense it is non-doing, but it also may become the most important thing that you do. So if you must do something, just sit there in your quiet corner.

Mindfulness throughout the Day

As you grow along your quiet-corner path, practicing your breathing, you will develop the skill to stay in the moment. At first, you might ask why this is so important. But as you progress, you will learn that this moment now is truly all there is. And if you are fully awake in this moment, everything is bliss. While this notion may sound like an exaggeration, the promise of it is worth the quest.

The skill to stay in the moment is first learned in your quiet corner. Practice it there and hone it so that you can take it with you and use it outside your quiet corner. Bring it to work with you. As you proceed through your day, pay attention to each task as you are working on it. Try not to sit in a meeting waiting for it to end. Handle each telephone call with your full attention. Bring it home with you. As you prepare supper, avoid thinking of how the food will taste and just be with the experience of cooking. Take a bath just to take a bath. Bring it into your leisure time. Without worrying about winning, play your tennis game, concentrating on each stroke. Plant the tomato plants without thought of eating their fruit.

The more mindful you become, the less stress you will experience. The more mindful you become, the more time you will seem to have. The more mindful you become, the less you will fear. The more mindful you become, the more acceptance you will have. Begin in your quiet corner, and slowly extend this new skill into your whole life. If spacing out in front of the TV or watching a movie is your way to relax, devote your full attention even to these activities and you will be more relaxed than usual. Take your life one moment at a time with your full attention, and you will never be disappointed.

Traveling with Your Quiet Corner

Whether you travel for business or pleasure, or both, a trip can be fraught with anxiety, pressure, and stress. Worrying about making a plane connection can ruin your two-hour flight. You will make it or not, and no amount of fretting will change that, so focus your attention on your breath and let the airline take care of the rest.

Lost luggage is one hazard of travel that very few people can accept with equanimity. But if you practice your quiet-corner skills as you discover the bad news, you might be surprised at how accepting you can be. Use this experience to observe yourself and how you handle this inconvenience. Will anger and public tantrums change the situation? Will they make you feel better? While almost no one is beyond getting upset, if you bring a little quiet corner onto the scene, your distress can be minimized. If you can find a quiet spot to retreat to for a few minutes, you will return a different person. Breathe and smile.

If you commute to work each day, whether by car or by public transportation, there are likely to be delays. Keep in mind that you are not at the center of the delay; you are not the cause, and you cannot change it. Here again, your quiet corner will come in handy. Sit if you can, breathe consciously, and enjoy the interlude.

So many of us view planes, trains, buses, and cars as simply a means of getting us from one place to another. If you are one of these people, try to change your outlook so that you can then gain the time that you once thought of as wasted, and use it to create more quiet corners in your life. You will no longer view travel time as a necessary evil. You may even begin to look forward to this time, just as you do to your time spent on the other end of the trip. Enjoy the time. It's a gift you didn't know you had.

Imperturbability

When I first started sitting in my quiet corner and was told to try to detach myself from my thoughts and my feelings, I thought I was being told not to think and feel. I expected to become an unfeeling, unthinking person. But at least, I thought, I would be more enlightened. So I marched on in my search for peace, trying not to feel or think. I didn't get very far and was convinced that I was a failure and would never know peace. But somewhere along the way, I learned that detachment from feelings and thoughts doesn't mean we have to stop feeling and thinking. We can no more stop feeling and thinking than we can stop breathing and still be alive and human. I now know it's okay to feel all our emotions and to think all our thoughts. The trick is not to be perturbed by them. Imperturbability is the goal of a quiet corner. And it is achievable. And it is worth the effort. And it may even make us more enlightened.

The big bonus here, once you learn to detach yourself from your thoughts and feelings, is that you will be less and less disturbed by the actions and feelings of others. You will be able to take in your stride anything that comes your way. And the bigger bonus, if you stay on the path and continue retreating to your quiet corner, is that you will also become less judgmental and more compassionate. I can't explain how detaching ourselves from our feelings makes us more capable of feeling for others, but it does. I will leave the explanation to the mystics. I only know the truth of this and, paradox or not, if imperturbability is possible and will, in turn, bring you to a joyful connection to your world, you'll be on the path for life.

The Payoff

While it may be admirable to approach any endeavor with no expectations and no need for reward, it's difficult to be human and not want something in return for our efforts. And although all the suggestions in this book are simple, they are not always easy. So I will now dangle a carrot in front of you and describe the rewards of following a quiet-corner path. These rewards will not magically appear just by reading this book. You must take the time and expend the effort. But if you do, you will not be disappointed. Simply keep your mind wherever you are and the path will be easier.

A life in balance will be yours. Physically, mentally, and emotionally, you will be in harmony with yourself and your surroundings. You will gain some insight into your life and your world. You will achieve clarity of mind. You will smile more and experience more joy. Peace and understanding will be yours. You will want less and be more appreciative of what you have. You will achieve a greater understanding of others and learn to love unconditionally.

All of this is possible if you simply take some time out, sit quietly, and breathe.

Part II

Serenity in Motion

INNER PEACE,

ANYTIME,

ANYWHERE

Introduction

The first part of this book, *Find a Quiet Corner,* originally published by itself, is an introduction to the practice of mindful breathing. It stresses the importance of setting aside time in your day to concentrate on this practice so that you can gain some peace of mind. There are many suggestions in it regarding how to find the time, where to set up your quiet corner, and what to do once you're there. *Serenity in Motion,* which was published next and comprises the second half of this book, builds on the practices developed in *Find a Quiet Corner* and brings them into the rest of your life.

The remedy for all your woes is very simple, but as you may know by now, it truly is not easy to put into practice. Some of you may have established a quiet corner at home to which you retreat at the beginning or end of your day in order to draw on your spiritual energy for guidance or to replenish the energy you've spent that day. Some of you who regularly find the time to spend in your quiet corner have reaped the rewards of this experience and live in harmony with the changing circumstances of your life. And some of you no longer resist what happens in your life and have come to welcome the unexpected. Yet you may find that spending time each day sitting quietly alone, focused on your breath, letting your thoughts float by without getting attached to them, doesn't always guarantee serenity. It can be threatened at any moment and in certain situations throughout the day. Sometimes, even before we are aware of it, we get caught in a whirlwind of actions or feelings that carries us into a storm of confusion. Our day gets upset, we blame ourselves or others, we project into the future, and we sit in disharmony until we can get back to our quiet corner and set ourselves back on course.

The good news is that you needn't wait to return to your quiet corner to reestablish your equanimity. You can carry the practices from your quiet corner into all of life's circumstances and employ them at any time. Thus, each day can be a rich and gratifying experience, where everything that happens is not only okay, but is exactly as it should be.

Just as it takes practice to hone the skills you learn in your quiet corner, so will it take practice to carry them with you and use them on all and sundry occasions as you face the daily vicissitudes of your life.

The complexity of our lives, the daily challenges that we encounter, and the myriad large and small decisions that we continually must make can challenge even the most serene of us. Yet even as we resist it, most of us are up to this challenge, because we intuitively know that we can rise above it all and not allow it to defeat us.

So let this book be your guide until you can tap into your own intuitive reservoir for all the solutions. In this section, you will find suggestions for dealing with some typical issues that might come your way on any given day. Keep in mind that it cannot cover every possible scenario. Your life is unique, as are your particular life's circumstances, not to mention the feelings and personality that you bring to everything. No one can know without a doubt what the future holds. In the end, it is up to you to meet each moment as it arrives, with honesty, integrity, and an open and willing heart.

All it takes is a decision. Not just one decision, but many throughout each day. Make a vow to yourself at the start of your day and renew it as often as necessary as the day progresses. This is the key to serenity. This is about accepting that each new moment is just that—new. And that no one moment can be duplicated exactly. This will give you a fresh start, a new opportunity to reinvent yourself every moment and live fully and completely, aware and awake, present in the magnanimous now.

Serenity in Motion is a primer for learning how to approach the world without reservation, fear, or self-imposed impediments. It is a tool to use while you train yourself to rely on yourself. Carry it with you, refer to it, and take the suggestions. Try new ways of looking at situations, of communicating with others, of seeing the world. Then start to take bigger risks and, finally, let your intuition guide you. Trust it. It will never fail you or let you down. And if you maintain a positive attitude, your worries will not overwhelm you. And most of all, remember to laugh. Simply laugh and be grateful for your life. In the end, it is all you have.

These are the main themes or threads running through *Serenity in Motion:*

- Embrace whatever it is that pains you.
- Loosen the tight hold you have on people, places, and things—good and bad.
- Just breathe.
- Expect nothing.
- Keep a positive attitude.
- Cultivate a sense of gratitude.
- Pay attention.
- Practice, practice, practice.

Some of these may seem contradictory, like embracing something only to then let it go. Think of it instead as a paradox that's not supposed to make logical sense. Right here, right now, is the perfect opportunity to practice these two suggestions. Here's how: Embrace your confusion; don't let it detain you or stop you from moving on. Allow yourself to be confused and then keep going. Once you've accepted your confusion, fully and completely, you no longer have a need to hold on. Just let go. Relax your grasp on it. And then notice how easy it is to let go once you've embraced it, compared to how impossible it was to resist it, push it away, and make it disappear.

Anytime you get stuck, refer to this simple exercise and practice it on the spot. Keep practicing it until it becomes second nature. Strive for perfection, but don't expect it. You may never reach perfection, but you will come to understand that the process itself is perfect.

BELLY-MIND

One other important concept woven throughout this section is that of *belly-mind,* often referred to as *hara,* which literally translates as "belly" or "gut." Many spiritual teachers throughout history have taught this concept in a variety of ways. Belly-mind is a "place" deep within us that guides us in spiritual matters. It is a place that defies logic and holds our answers. Some say it is the seat of intuition. In the Zen tradition, *hara* is said to be our center of gravity, awareness, and energy, located about two inches below our navel. It is the center that holds your inner truth, the center that is home for your spirit, the center from which serenity arises.

Nothing can be done without using the muscles in our abdomen. When we cry, laugh, fight, or make love, we use these muscles. Whenever we move a body part or exert energy of any sort, we must use our abdominal muscles. Belly-mind is based on the principle that when we create tension in our bellies, and concentrate our energy there, we create physical and mental stability. Breathing deeply into our bellies can also control our thoughts and habitual reactions. The breath draws attention to the *hara* and away from ego-driven thought. This focused mindfulness generates all the spiritual power that you need to be in a continual state of alert and wakeful serenity, where nothing is "wrong" and everything makes sense.

At all times, whether sitting or moving around, concentrate on this place in your body. Breathe from there, think from there, and move from there. Retrain your first brain into thinking of this gut feeling or "second brain" as its master. Imagine that you are carrying around a red-hot ball of fire located in your belly just below your navel. When your attention strays from there and rises up, immediately drop it back down to this center of gravity by using your breath as the transport. Think of it as a life-and-death matter—you must operate from this place no matter what.

Although it is not easy to be concentrated on your belly every second while sitting still, it is even more challenging to do it while moving around. Right now, as you read these words, draw them into your belly. Focus completely on your belly until you are just one big belly brain, breathing and laughing through to the end of this page and then on to the rest of your day.

Don't settle for less than total belly absorption. Commit yourself to this practice. Make a vow to yourself right now that you will carry belly-mind into everything that you do, think, feel, see, hear, say, smell, and breathe. Trust the spiritual teachers who have come before you and identified this belly-mind as your spiritual center; trust also that your troubles are spiritual maladies that have spiritual solutions.

If you are dedicated, and if you carry this mindful practice with you twenty-four hours a day, there is no question that you will have a contented, meaningful life. Trust that. And if you don't trust yet, allow yourself to doubt, and breathe that into your belly. Breathe in the doubt and breathe out trust. If you truly want meaning and serenity in your life, live from your belly.

The Practice of Being Still

We can be moving at a furious pace even when we're not in motion. This activity is usually our mind working overtime, which can cause stress, distress, anxiety, and health problems. The solution then is simple: Slow down the movement of our mind.

But when our mind continues to move, even after our body is quiet, it can keep us from making the effort to be still, which moves us even further away from a calm mind. Our mind keeps chattering once we've stilled our body, because our mind doesn't want us to be still. When we are still, our mind inevitably slows down and is no longer in charge. But our mind, and most especially our petty ego, wants to be in charge; it is not happy when it's not, so it does everything in its power to keep us moving. And it usually wins.

So then the question becomes, how do we take charge of our mind? You might also wonder, isn't my mind me? If I'm not in charge of my own mind, then who or what is? Good questions. Put them aside for a moment and consider this: If you were truly in charge of your mind, wouldn't you just be able to say to it, calm down, relax, don't worry, stop thinking so much, and other similar things? Haven't we all tried such coaxing? Has it ever worked?

So now what? Well, the good news is that there is a way to take charge. Rather than fighting fire with fire, pitting will against will, you can learn another approach to relieve the pressure, quiet your mind, and let go of the need for answers.

What is this miraculous way? What do we use, if not our will, to calm ourselves and become masters of our minds?

Breath—it's really that simple. Almost too simple for our complicated minds to understand and accept.

It may seem like there must be more to it, but the answer is, not really.

It is simply a matter of concentrating and bringing your attention to your breath. The key concept here is concentration. This is where your indomitable will can be utilized. Draw all of your energy and spirit into each breath, and as you do, draw your breath deeper and deeper into your belly-mind. Each time your mind strays, gently draw it back as you would a windblown scarf, and concentrate with all your might and attention on each inhalation and each exhalation. This is not an easy task. Each time, thoughts and sounds and disappointments will disturb you. But there will come a point when you will experience, for a fraction of a second, such full concentration on your breathing that all thoughts and outside interference will halt. This "space between thoughts" is where your truth resides, where your essence is revealed. Eventually, with practice, these moments will get longer, and you will completely lose yourself in the practice of concentrated breathing, deep in your belly. Then you will know why this practice is so valuable. You will experience contentment as never before, and a deep understanding will prevail. But even before this, when you engage in this concentrated breath practice each day, for fifteen, twenty, forty minutes, a number of things happen:

- Your body slows down.
- Your breath gets deeper.
- Your mind follows and begins to slow down (sometimes kicking and screaming, but eventually giving in peacefully).

- Your heart rate slows.
- Anger, depression, and anxiety abate.
- Pain symptoms subside.

These things occur, plus much more. You have the power to manifest these benefits. So concentrate, keep a positive attitude, and breathe your way to serenity.

As you become more aware of your breath, you will naturally cultivate a spirit of gratitude for your breath, because it equals life. Prior to this breath-attention practice, you most likely took your breath for granted, but do no longer. Once you stop taking your life-source for granted, you will extend this same attitude to all other things and people and circumstances. You might have to remind yourself now and then, but if you keep up the breath-awareness practice, then the practice of gratitude will automatically follow.

LISTENING

How many of us know how to really listen? Do we know how to listen to our own mind as it careens out of control and races off on some tangent or other, into the past or the future? Or to others—our coworkers, loved ones, or strangers—as they attempt to communicate something to us? To the everyday sights, sounds, and sensations that surround us? Even if we think of ourselves as good listeners, and are seen that way by others, it is wise to be open to the idea that there is always more to learn, that there are deeper levels of hearing we can access.

The practice of listening can be done anywhere at any time. Opportunities to hone your listening skills are presented to you throughout each day. All that is required is to still yourself and pay attention. Once you decide to really listen, bring your whole body into the activity, not just your ears and your brain. You do this naturally anyway, but I invite you to witness yourself doing it and then expand upon this power. The very next time you hear a pleasant sound—a child's laugh or a church bell—stop and pay attention; breathe it into you. Listen to it with your gut, your belly, even your toes. Do it right now as you read this. Listen to the room sounds in this way. Do the same thing with an unpleasant sound—police sirens or traffic noise. First, notice your reaction and resistance to it, your impulse to will it away, and how that affects your body. Then invite the sound in (what other choice do you have?) and notice the difference. Rather than let any sound, pleasant or unpleasant, become a distraction, allow it to be part of your environment, part of your personal space. Be with the sounds, move with them, and give up the battle to control them.

Here's an exercise that can be practiced every time you exchange words with someone else.

First, as they speak to you, notice your reaction to their words. Are you thinking about how their message affects you, how to respond to them, or what they need from you? Do you find yourself interjecting comments or gestures to signal to them that you're listening? How much of your listening is about you rather than about them?

Second, experiment with the notion that it's okay for you to say nothing. Then just listen and curb your desire to jump in, to assert yourself. Wait until they've said all they want to say before you speak. If there's silence, as they struggle to formulate an idea or reach for some word, let the silence be okay. Don't rush to fill it. Practice being silent and just listening.

Engage a friend in this listening exercise: Take turns

speaking and listening. Choose a topic to talk about—your boss, your partner, a recent experience, or a career ambition—and then spend five minutes listening, as your friend speaks, and five minutes speaking, as your friend listens. When you listen, just listen—in stillness and in silence. In no time, you will see that when you free yourself of the obligation to respond, not only do you become a better listener, but also your friend feels heard in a new and expansive way.

STANDING

Standing still is anathema to so many these days. Our lives are about movement, about doing, about getting someplace. We so rarely are where we are. Instead, we're into the next thing, place, thought, or action, before we even get there. And then when we do get there, we hardly take the time to be there, as we're off into the next whatever. We are racing to catch up with ourselves, which usually leaves us stressed out and short of breath, hoping everything will stop and wondering when relief will come. We even chase after relief, even though it is eternally out of reach when we do pursue it.

If this is all true, it seems that the solution is to just stop. But because this is nearly impossible to contemplate, let alone accomplish, we feel defeated before we even begin. We've tried slowing down before with little success. The surprise here is that you are already doing what you need to do and the only thing now is to take advantage of those already existing moments.

Standing, at the bus stop, the copier, or the ATM, in the theater or the grocery store checkout line; waiting for the elevator to arrive or the stoplight to change—throughout the day, we frequently find ourselves standing with no place to go, and too often we squander this time. Anxious for movement, we view the stillness, the lack of motion, as a waste of time. Paradoxically, when we're on life's treadmill, all we want to do is stop. Yet when we do, we yearn to move. This is just one example of never being satisfied with where we are.

All it takes to transform these moments from dreadful to delightful is a little mind movement, a shift in attitude. Even if you cannot change to a new outlook directly, if you're reading this, you most likely have the willingness to take a different approach. And if you're willing, then change is possible.

When your body comes to a standstill, your mind doesn't always follow right away, which is why not moving can create such internal discomfort. So when you find yourself standing still with your mind on fast forward, there are two things you can do.

First of all, you can become aware of your body in space, where it is, how it feels. Notice your posture and any tension you might have in your spine. Make slight adjustments to how you're standing, and breathe into your whole back, as you center your awareness on the fact that you are able to stand upright. Feel your feet standing firmly on the ground. Imagine that there are roots solidly planting you into the earth, your legs the trunk of a tree, your upper body the branches gently swaying in the breeze. If you're carrying heavy bags, place them down as you stand there, unburdened and free. Appreciate your body; savor the moment. Be there with every inch of every fiber of your being.

Then, once you've stilled your body, observe your mind and where it wants to take you physically, mentally, and emotionally. Watch your thoughts; simply stand there, breathe into your belly, be in your body, and pay attention—without judgment or criticism. Consider that everyone around you, standing with you, contains a similarly active mind. It might take time, but know that if you still your body, the mind will eventually follow and reach a state of stillness—the first step to serenity.

And keep in mind that there are no needless, wasted moments. Each one is precious and an opportunity to experience contentment. So stand tall in your life with all that it offers, good and bad, and know that serenity is available in and through everything. Be sure to stand wherever you are and you won't miss it.

SITTING

Although we may find ourselves sitting down through much of the day, how many of us ever make a conscious decision just to sit? Usually, when we're sitting, we are also driving or eating or working or watching a movie or relaxing. Sitting is usually about something other than just sitting. And if we've ever contemplated the idea of sitting for the sake of sitting, perhaps we've concluded that it would be a simple waste of time—so even if we've been advised to do it, we often choose not to. Just the thought of sitting and doing nothing may terrify us, especially when it's linked to the word *meditation*. Take this moment to discard all your preconceived notions of what sitting still is all about. Drop the word *meditation* from your vocabulary. And then allow yourself to be open to sitting in a new way.

Just sitting—here, you will find the source for your serenity. Just sitting—here, you will develop a practice of being still that you can then bring into all your other activities. Just sitting—this is the only suggestion in this book that it's best not to skip.

So take a seat with the clear intention to just sit. Begin

with five or ten minutes, and use your body and your breath to do it. Let your mind come along for the ride, or in this case, the "sit." Concentrate on your posture (erect), your breathing (deep and slow), and your fingers and toes (relaxed). Begin each session with closed eyes in order to draw your attention inward. Then once you're focused, gently open your eyes and just breathe. There's nothing to do, nowhere to go. Watch as your mind tries to pull you away from any discomfort you might experience. Breathe deeply into your belly. Expect nothing. Simply and gently, just sit and breathe. Practice being still. The longer you still your body and the deeper into your belly you breathe, the quieter your mind will become. This practice of sitting still and doing nothing will eventually create space between thoughts. This space will hold pure, intrinsic awareness. This will be the breeding ground for serenity—not just as you sit, but at all times. So sit still and discover this internal mechanism for creating peace and harmony within, no matter what is going on outside. Then you can carry it with you always and tap into it whenever you need it.

WAITING

Waiting—we all do it. We wait for the movie to start, the train to come, the weekend, our vacation. We can't wait until we meet the "right" partner, we're in the perfect job, or we have more money. What we're really doing in all these situations is waiting for our life to happen. We're waiting for the next thing, biding our time. It isn't your fault, you might say, "the train isn't here yet" or "I'm so unhappy in my job." Perhaps, but consider this: The train may never come. Then what? Your life will have been about just waiting. If this idea doesn't appeal to you, then you can begin to transform your waiting time into being-present time.

One way to convert the "waiting" into "being" is with language. All it takes is some willingness and then awareness. Each time you notice yourself using the word *wait*, change it to something else. For instance, "I'm waiting for the train; it's late again" can be changed to "I'm at the train station. My train isn't on schedule. That gives me time to read without distraction. What a gift." This is an example of a shift from negative, biding-time language to positive, present-moment language. Feel the difference? And once your language changes, your attitude and behavior will change. And then peace of mind will be close at hand.

Usually, we get irritated if we find ourselves waiting for something or someone, because we feel duped. We did not schedule the waiting time into our day, we are in a hurry to get to the next thing, and we feel at the mercy of some outside force, all of which makes us feel like victims. But if we can see the flip side of this and admit that it is not something being done to us, it is just something that happens, we can then react in a more positive way and use it to our advantage.

Waiting can be an opportunity, a gift of time, to spend constructively, frivolously, or however else you choose. Use it to do the crossword puzzle or read that magazine you never have time to otherwise. Daydream or write a love letter that you may never send. Strike up a conversation with a stranger. Not to pass the time, but to be present in time. Notice how time expands when you're waiting for something else to happen. The seconds seem to tick by more slowly than usual. Rather than defining this as lost time, see it as found time, as time that moves slowly, time that you can be in and savor.

Once you rephrase your approach to this waiting period, settle down into it and let the power of it, the gift of it, wash over you and create stillness in your mind. You will see how easy this is to do once you do it the first time. Coax your mind back from its destination—where you expected to be once the "waiting" is over—and be present in your current circumstances. You will learn soon enough that you can't be anywhere else. So why not be here and enjoy it? Otherwise, one day your life will be over and you won't remember how you got there.

WATCHING TV

When you watch television, do you do it mindlessly, hoping to relax and put out of your mind the travails of the day? Do you ever sit for hours in front of the tube to escape your usual life? Do you do it for lack of something else to do? Do you always have it on in the background even if you're not sitting and watching it? Do you sometimes feel guilty after watching it, sure that you could have spent the time more productively?

Whatever your answers to these questions may be, the bottom line is that if you have a TV in your house, you have a relationship with it. If you don't have a TV, you can substitute your computer, CD player, radio, or telephone here. In any case, your relationship with your appliances can be improved by employing the tools of mindfulness and concentration, two tools that we will be using throughout this book to nurture serenity and contentedness.

We'll look at mindfulness first. If there's a particular show you're fond of or you want to wind down from your day, make the decision to watch TV and set the time aside exclusively for this purpose. Consciously choosing to turn it on and watch, rather than slipping into an old habitual pattern, is the first step to mindful viewing. Then sit down and just watch the program. Don't eat, read, clean, or do anything else as you watch TV. Mindfully pay attention to what you are watching, to where you are sitting as you watch, to how you're feeling, and what your enjoyment level is.

Then concentrate on just watching your show. No strain or exertion. Simply concentrate on what you've chosen to do. Be there with the TV, just you and it. Even if family members are watching with you, this can still be your exercise, with you and the TV. No one else need even know what you're doing.

Spend a week or two mindfully concentrating on this activity of sitting still and just watching. Take notice of the various realizations that arise in connection with this practice. Are you enjoying TV more or less this way? Does it make you want to watch more or less often? What have you discovered about yourself vis-à-vis your habits of television watching?

This practice is not intended to curb or increase the time you spend watching TV. It is meant merely to guide you toward consciously and mindfully choosing when and what to watch so that your serenity is not compromised. Once you know what works best for you, give yourself permission to occasionally indulge in some mindless TV watching, just so long as you mindfully make that choice. Give yourself the freedom not to punish yourself or feel guilty, and then, enjoy.

BEING PATIENT

No matter how quickly we want things to change or how much we want things, people, or situations to be different than they are or how much we want, period, the wisest choice is usually to do nothing. This is the ultimate being-still practice. Doing nothing seems like just that: nothing. Perhaps on the surface it looks that way, but when we do nothing there is a lot going on. This something is called life.

Consider the word *life* for just a moment. What is it? See if you can detach from what you call your life and become an observer, a detached anthropologist of what it is you call your life. Can you see that you cannot know how events in your life will evolve? Can you see that your life has energy with or without your hands on the controls and that it usually goes much more smoothly if you let go? Can you feel the calm that results from stepping aside for these few moments as you observe this phenomenon called your life, and let life live you rather than you living life?

If you do not experience these things right away, do not worry. Practicing the patience to let life events unfold on their own will give you an opportunity to truly participate in your life rather than continually trying to control the outcome, the results, and the solution. And this practice will lead to equanimity and a life filled with life. Ask yourself, what more could you want? As you continue to practice patience, you will know that all is as it should be and your job is simply to show up and ask each day how you can be of service to yourself, your loved ones and others, and your life. And remember that all answers will be revealed, as my spiritual teacher is fond of saying, "with the readiness of time."

To put it another way, being patient is simply this: just being and expecting nothing.

The Practice of Being in Motion

There is a grave misconception that serenity can only be had while meditating and that meditation can only be done in a quiet room with no distractions. Many people think that meditation is a break from life, a mind vacation, a time-out from the usual, and that if we do this, if we take these breaks, then the rest of our life will run smoothly.

While there is some truth to this, mostly it's an unbalanced view of what meditation is and how it can work in our lives. The most important thing to know is that meditation is not a withdrawal from life; it is an extension of it. And while it is crucial to sit still, as described in the previous section, if we limit our opportunities for spiritual growth and serenity to the times when we are still, we will be doing ourselves a disservice, especially since most of our time is spent other than sitting still.

Sitting still is merely the foundation for building a complete life of serenity. We cannot do without it. But just as a foundation alone does not make a home, sitting still by itself does not make a serene life. And just as a house will crumble and fall without a foundation, so will our life if we do not practice sitting still. But there is more to a calm mind than just sitting still. Once we begin our sitting-still practice, we can then take what we learn there and apply it everywhere else. The first place we can use it—the place where we are most of the time—is the place of being in motion. And being in motion and approaching it as practice is a lovely way to engage with life and nurture your serenity.

The most vital element of this practice is mindfulness. In the practice of being still, you learned about concentration, about paying attention, about listening, about constantly bringing yourself back to your breath, your belly-mind, or to other being-still moments. This is the beginning of mindfulness. So many of us reside either in the past or in the future. We obsess about what did or didn't happen or what will or won't happen next. Our minds become filled with worry or anxiety. Mindfulness is the cure to an overflowing, chattering, busy mind. With mindfulness, we simply draw our attention to the present moment, activity, or feeling. We pay attention to what is happening right now by concentrating on the action itself. Lose yourself in what you are doing. Get rid of the idea "I am doing" or "I am feeling" and just do, just feel. When you are self-conscious, you cannot concentrate on anything. Freedom from self-consciousness through mindfulness allows for a creative and productive moment, day, and life.

When mindfulness is practiced, thoughts of the past or the future begin to recede and you become present to what is happening now. When you are present, your life does not pass you by as you wait for it to happen. It happens as you live it. It cannot be any other way. The truth and power of this will be revealed as soon as you begin to practice mindfulness. You can do this any place, at any time—being still or being in motion. And from this, you can build your own temple of serenity.

WALKING

Buddha said of himself and his monks: "When we walk, we know we are walking." This is a beautiful practice and one of the simplest and most immediately rewarding and instructive. It is both grounding and freeing. The benefits suit our need for immediate gratification, because they begin to appear with the first step. And they are endless. All you have to do is be present with each step.

Rather than focus on your destination, gather yourself with each breath and bring your attention to the activity of walking. Set some time aside to spend just walking, or each time you find yourself walking from one place to the next, be mindful of what you are doing and put out of your mind where you are going. Bring your awareness to the walking, and put aside the idea that it is a means to an end. If you can be there, present, alert, and mindful, as you take steps and move your body across the earth and through space, then you will be there for your life. This is not a race to the end—even if some days it may feel that way. It is just life and yours at that.

So whether you set time aside to just walk or you take advantage of the various times throughout the day when you're walking, do it mindfully. Begin by counting your steps, one-to-ten, one-to-ten, and so on. This will bring your attention into your body, into the act of walking. Then, as you continue to count your steps, bring your attention to your breath. Don't alter your step or your breath; just draw all your attention to them. Notice how many steps you take on each inhale, on each exhale. Notice your impulse to stop, to think of where you're going, to move faster, and then just count and breathe. As your rhythm modulates, count the steps you take on each inhalation and each exhalation. Inhale, one-two-three. Exhale, one-two-three. Just notice, breathe, and count. Start to become aware of the surrounding environment. Be in it, be present, and be mindful. It is not about how fast or slow you move; it is only about being present in each step you take. Move toward having the number of steps you take on the inhalation equal the number of steps you take on the exhalation. And then every so often take an extra step on the exhale and lengthen your exhalation.

If you discover that you move so fast through life that mindful walking is nearly impossible, because each time you make the effort to slow down your body your mind continues to speed ahead, do not be discouraged. Do not, at first, intentionally slow your physical movement. Keep your normal pace, and within that movement, little by little, start to pay attention to your breath, to each step. You may not be able to sustain mindful attention the whole distance from your house to the car or bus, but if a portion of that walk is taken mindfully, it is a good beginning. Each day add one more breath to this mindfulness practice. Be patient and trust that if you walk with your body your mind will eventually follow. Both will reach a calm place if you continue the practice. So just walk and let each moment reveal its unique mystery. Then, each time you walk, you will know that you are walking.

TALKING

Paying attention to the words we use and the effect they have on others, ourselves, and on our own level of serenity is just the beginning of using this everyday activity to bring tranquility into each day. Just as we can adopt good and bad habits of behavior, so can we do this with our patterns of speech. At times, we are completely unaware of what we are saying. Paying attention is crucial.

There are two aspects to this talk practice, one being deconstructive, the other constructive.

When your serenity is disturbed after you have had a conversation with someone, deconstruct what happened. Review what it was that you said, and think about how you would change it if you could have the conversation again. Of course, you won't get a second chance, but new opportunities to talk in a different way will continue to arise. Don't get caught in the trap of feeling that the other person's words should be different—you have no control over that. Over time, notice your speech patterns and decide to use your words differently on the next occasion presented to you. Perhaps you will notice that you say too much or too little or that your tone is blaming or hostile. Maybe you will notice that you use self-defeating or self-deprecating language. Whatever it is, do not judge it; simply decide that you'd like to change it.

On the constructive side of this talk practice, when you're engaged in conversation use positive, upbeat language. Do not lie, gossip, or engage in frivolous conversation. This may seem like a tall order, and you may not even be aware that you do it. Every one of us is probably guilty of it at times. While it may seem like innocent fun, keep in mind that words are very powerful and it is your responsibility to use language wisely. It isn't necessary to be self-righteous when others attempt to seduce you into gossip. Simply change the subject or communicate that you'd rather not participate in the conversation. Or just walk away without casting judgment.

When you have nothing useful to say, keep a "noble silence." Bring the practice of listening into this practice of talking. Let silence be an integral part of the whole experience. As soon as idle chatter falls away, you will be more attentive to the person you are talking to and to yourself. Talking will become more meaningful. No words will be wasted. No unnecessary chatter will clutter the atmosphere, and serenity will prevail.

EATING

This is another truly delightful mindfulness practice. In the Zen Buddhist tradition, meals are ritualized and taken in silence. Chants that invite mindfulness and gratitude are recited, and no one begins eating until everyone is served. Only as much as can be eaten is taken. No one goes hungry. No one overeats. During the meal, everyone pays attention to just eating. At the conclusion of the meal, there is more chanting as everyone is reminded of his or her purpose for the day and in life.

This beautiful practice can be easily adapted to our hectic Western lives. Here's how:

• **Plan your meals.**
You know the needs of your body better than anyone does. Whether you need frequent, small meals throughout the day or do best with the usual three, it is important to schedule them.

• **Confine your eating to mealtimes.**
If your body needs nourishment in the afternoon between formal meals, plan that into your meal schedule; even if it's not a full meal, consider it as important as the others.

• **Do not eat on the run.**
It is dangerous both nutritionally and otherwise to eat while driving or walking or doing anything else. But be flexible. There are times when we need to break the rules.

• **Make a ritual of it.**
Set the table, light a candle, say a prayer. Do whatever fits your personality. Create your own meaningful eating practice. Include your family and friends.

• **Turn off the TV and just eat.**

It's okay to have a conversation while eating; in fact, it's a great time for families to come together and share their plans or their experiences of the day. But let there be no other distractions. Be together (or alone) and just eat. Serve yourself only what you're sure you'll eat. Be mindful not to waste food. Bring a sense of gratitude to the simple fact that you have enough (probably more than enough) to eat.

If you are the one who cooks, take this same mindful approach to the preparation of the food. When chopping, just chop; when stirring, just stir. The meal will then be infused with your mindful energy, which will then be transmitted to those who eat what you have lovingly prepared.

So, when eating, just eat. And in so doing, be like Buddha.

PLAYING

You might wonder why there's a section here on play. This probably seems like one area of your life where you don't need help. This is where you know how to be present, mindful, happy, and serene. This is where, whether it be during a tennis or Monopoly game, while running or bowling, you've experienced losing yourself and just playing. Even if you don't take the time out very often anymore, even if you have to summon childhood memories, you do know how to play and enjoy it. You don't need to be taught a thing.

There are only two things to say here. One, play as often as you can. And two, take what you know in this realm of your life and apply it elsewhere.

While at play, we can be both serious (we want to play our best and win) and lighthearted (it's about having fun and not the end of the world if we lose), and we can get so completely absorbed that we become "one" with whatever it is we're playing. But if playing has become so serious a pursuit for you that there are times when it's not fun, then it's time to look at that and begin to change it.

Go back to a time in your life when you weren't so serious, when playing was what it's supposed to be. Bring that child mind into your present-day play activities. Then when play is once again fun, bring this mindset into other areas of your life. Carry a sense of play to work with you, into your relationships, and out into the community. Whenever you begin a new and challenging project, approach it in a balanced, playful way, with a serious yet lighthearted attitude. This may take some practice and you'll never be "perfect." But isn't that what play is all about? Focus on loving the doing of it as you love the playing of play. Put the consequences out of your mind, and just be in the moment-to-moment engagement.

As you develop your habits of mindfulness, your self-awareness will increase. So whenever you become aware that you are in a much more solemn mood than the occasion calls for, or you are taking things much too personally, take a moment to regroup your faculties and encourage your mind to enter into a play mode. In other words, lighten up.

Play always utilizes the body. Go for a fast walk or a run around the block to help you shift gears. Notice that when your mind is serious and self-involved, your body is most likely tense or highly agitated. When you move your body, you will stir your mind. And then laughter, or at least a deep smile, will be possible. Anytime you get close to this, you are that much closer to serenity. So call a friend who makes you laugh or read something funny and transform your too-serious mood into a more playful one. Just by way of a smile, your whole attitude and outlook will change.

TASKING

If you're a typical, modern human being with too much to do and not enough time to do it all, you probably spend a considerable amount of time just thinking about what you have to do before you actually do it. Let's first look at the thinking half of this process. You already know that obsessive thinking can disrupt your peace of mind by projecting you into a future that hasn't yet arrived. Anxiety builds up as you worry about all that you have to do and when you might do it. Because it's impossible to do all those things at once, and because you cannot accomplish anything just by thinking about it, you begin to feel overwhelmed before you even begin.

As soon as you recognize that your mind has moved forward in time, bring yourself gently back to the present by taking a few deep breaths and noticing where you are. What color is the wall or the sky in front of you? Who are you with? What are they wearing? Even if you are surrounded by strangers, observe their different forms of dress. Then re-focus on whatever it is you were doing and know that the chores ahead of you will get done when you get to them. If your mind continues to project ahead into thinking about all you have to do, and you can't concentrate on the present moment, take out your notebook and write a daily task list, a weekly task list, a monthly task list, and a sometime-in-the-future task list. If you have time, prioritize each list. Then put the notebook away and return to what you were doing.

Now let's look at the doing side of this process. When you get to the doing of the first chore on your list later that day, or the next, bring your full attention to it. If it's the laundry, concentrate completely on separating the colors from the whites, on loading the machine, on setting the dial, on hanging up or folding each article of clothing. Bring to this chore a feeling of gratitude for the fact that you have clothes to wash and a machine to wash them in. Be grateful for the running water and electricity that make this chore possible and quite simple. Involve yourself 100 percent in this activity. If you notice that you are thinking ahead to the completion of the task, pull yourself gently back to whatever your hands are doing in this moment and imagine what you would be feeling if you were doing it for the very first time. Open your heart to the miracle of your hands and feet and legs and whatever else you are utilizing to accomplish this chore, and be grateful for your ability to complete this task.

Whether it is washing the dishes, sweeping the floor, raking the leaves, or building a tree house, bring your complete and focused attention to the doing of it. Each time your mind wanders, gently coax it back. When you are engaged in doing a chore that has been particularly distasteful to you in the past, use the opportunity to learn more about yourself. Bring yourself back to the first time you did this chore or to the time when it turned sour for you. Forgive whomever or whatever it was that you believe responsible for your present attitude (even, or most especially, if it's you), and remove all the emotional baggage from the current-day task at hand. And then do it as if for the first time and shift your negative attitude into a positive one.

Since it's not always easy to go directly to a positive outlook, use the practice of mindfulness to take you there—be utterly and completely in the present moment, in the doing of the task at hand. When cleaning, just clean; when cooking, just cook; when raking, just rake. This practice will encourage positive thinking and prepare you for the ultimate task of just *being*. Do the chore to do the chore, nothing more. And in the doing of it, just *be*.

DRIVING

Like riding a bicycle, once we learn how to drive a car, our body remembers and we no longer have to think about it. On automatic pilot, we start the car, shift into gear, step on the gas, and off we go. Of course, we check the mirror, look over our shoulder, and watch for oncoming traffic, but all of this is done as reflex action. Once we are on the road with the cruise control on, our mind searches for something to do. So we pick up the phone or eat our lunch or listen to the radio. But what if you took this time to just sit and just drive, in silence?

Pay attention to your body in the seat, your outstretched arms, and your hands on the wheel. Check your breathing. Consciously slow it down and deepen it, silently saying "deep" on the inhalation and "slow" on the exhalation. Be attentive to the traffic flow, the hum of your car, the wind in your hair, being still and being in motion simultaneously. This is another opportunity for serenity in motion. Many of us easily slip into the mindless version of this, which can be very dangerous, and all it takes to turn it into mindful driving is to employ some of the tools you've learned so far.

Even if you haven't expressed road rage or leaned heavily on the horn in an attempt to move traffic forward, chances are you have experienced some frustration behind the wheel of your car. While driving mindfully and serenely on an open road is possible and appealing, most of our time is usually spent in the more stop-and-go local traffic situations that are ripe for sowing irritation. Usually, we are in a hurry to get someplace, and the red lights always seem to be against us. We often end up behind a student or a seemingly inexperienced driver. We want an explanation for the traffic jam. We lose our patience. We lose our temper. Our mind becomes engaged in the futile task of willing circumstances to change. Any serenity we had going in gets completely shot. Whew! We're out of breath just thinking about it.

Given that you cannot change the traffic, the first thing you can do is let go of your desire to do that. Accept the situation as it is presented to you. Take advantage of this time to generate mindfulness. Be completely present to your body sitting in your car on Main Street. Notice the time, the slant of the sun, and the other drivers' faces. Be aware of your need to change how it is at this moment. Relax into being frustrated, being slowed down, and finally into being you. Acknowledge that the other drivers around you are probably feeling some frustration as well. Send them some positive energy. Smile at them. Share the experience of being there. Laugh at your collective predicament. And then when you finally get to your destination (and remember, you can't get there until you get there), you will be relaxed and ready for the next thing, in harmony with everything as it occurs.

The city version of the above might take place sitting on the edge of the bus or cab seat, willing the traffic to move faster or the driver to drive the way you would if only you were driving. The first thing to remember is that you're not in control of how the traffic flows or the driver drives. Then it's just a small step to sitting back and enjoying the ride.

BATHING

There are certain daily practices that we all engage in to maintain our physical and mental health, with eating, sleeping, and bathing being the three main ones. Whether you're mindful of it or not, most likely you already have established habits of bathing. It is probably a daily act that takes place at about the same time, at least five days a week. You may have a set routine in how you wash your body—top to bottom, or vice versa. Chances are this activity has become such an ingrained habit that you don't have to think about it. This allows you to wander off in your mind and look ahead at what might be waiting for you the rest of the day.

Most of us also take for granted the fact that we have hot running water and rarely consider that water itself is becoming a scarce commodity. While every activity is an opportunity to practice mindfulness, bathing is especially perfect because we can usually arrange to be alone, there is little to distract us but our own mind, and it feels good. Begin to transform your bathing experience from mindless to mindful by establishing a ritual. Do it in silence. Bring all your attention into the bathroom. Establish a new pattern of washing your body and be attentive to each detail. Draw your mind to each body part as you wash it. Without luxuriating in the feel of the water, be mindful of its pure quality and direct your mind into an attitude of gratitude. (Luxuriating in a hot tub of scented water surrounded by candles and soft music is a different experience and one to be taken every so often, if you are so inclined. It can be a mindfully relaxing time and quite different from your daily bathing routine.)

Each time you bathe is an opportunity to practice mindfulness and establish gratitude—a good start to your day. It can also be one of the times each day when you remind yourself of the third leg of the tripod of contentedness: spiritual health. Along with physical and mental health, your spiritual condition determines how grounded and content you will be in your body and in your life. Too often, this third leg gets neglected so that our serenity becomes wobbly and unstable. Rather than seek a spiritual solution, we often resort to shoring up the other two legs by eating or sleeping more, which further destabilizes our condition. Just as healthy eating practices determine our physical health and sound sleep contributes to our mental health, let your bathing practice be one of the ways you confirm your commitment to spiritual health. As part of your ritual, before stepping into the tub or shower, make a vow to yourself to be completely present as you bathe. Then just wash your body as you begin practicing mindfulness. When finished, seal the experience with another vow to continue this mindfulness practice throughout the day.

And remember that every suggestion in this book is merely a suggestion. If you are committed to living a mindful, serene life, you will take what works for you, discard the rest, and create your own unique ways of keeping your tripod of serenity healthy.

WORKING

It's unfortunate that the routine of working has such a bad rap these days. Since we spend the bulk of our day working, our attitude toward it determines our level of harmony in relation to it. So if we are stuck in negativity—blaming our boss, the job itself, and the long hours we spend at work for our distress—no matter how our work evolves, we will stay stuck until we shift our attitude. The bad news here is that it's entirely up to you—not your boss, your situation, or the money you make—to change.

The good news is that it's entirely up to you. You and only you have the power to transform the effect work has on you.

Only you can transform a feeling of dread when going to work into joyful anticipation. Sometimes you may discover that nothing short of leaving your job and moving on to something else is the answer. But most of the time all you need to do is adopt a positive attitude. This may not happen all at once and it may not happen naturally. So the way to get to a positive attitude is one step at a time, one task at a time.

Bring your full attention—your entire body, mind, and spirit—into the *doing* of each work activity. If your task is dependent on someone else and that person is not cooperating, move on to the next thing, rather than getting caught in the web of griping and waiting and, hence, not working. When you notice yourself thinking about coming to the end of what you're doing or about how nice it will be to finish work for the day, bring yourself back to the project at hand and be unconditionally in the *doing* of it. If your to-do list or in-box or some unfinished business or unpleasant task is gnawing at you to be done, take the time to do it, mindfully, respectfully, and diligently. Leave the negative attitude out of it. Just make the phone call, write the letter, or file those papers—whatever it is. And it will be done. It will no longer take up space in your mind. Thus, you will start to create new work habits, and you'll begin to feel better about each job and about yourself as a worker. Positive thinking will begin to replace negative thinking, and your attitude will naturally lean toward the positive without having to take any giant leap. You will exult in the doing of whatever it is you must do whenever it is you must do it. *Work* will no longer be a bad word and something outside of you; it will become intrinsic to who you are. Your life will be a seamless flow of positive energy with work an integral part. All you have to do right now is turn the page and the rest will follow.

The Practice of Being Challenged

Just getting through a typical day without ending up exhausted or embittered can sometimes be so daunting that when faced with some of the larger challenges of life we seem to have no energy left for the fight. So we let the major events take control and toss us to and fro, all the while thinking that we have no choice. But we do have a choice. We can face all the challenges that life serves us, big and small, maintaining our serenity in the process. We can learn to roll with the punches so that nothing takes us by surprise and we stay on course even when the turbulent winds blow.

At this point, you've established a foundation built on concentration and mindfulness. Together, with these, you can now engage some energy to see you through the challenging times and situations that are bound to arise. When you set time aside—even if it's only ten minutes a day—to be still and concentrate on your breath, your energy reserves will continually be replenished and you'll be able to summon up some energy whenever it's needed. This will allow you to work with determination through each challenge as it appears. It is important to keep in mind here that when you are committed to this practice, you will never be given more than you can handle in any given day. Trust that. You have the resources. You have the power. You have the energy to face all challenges and come to the other side—whole, serene, and content in the knowledge that you stepped up to the plate and gave it your all.

Once you begin the practice of being challenged, you will even come to view challenges as opportunities rather than obstacles. You will be empowered by them and shrink from nothing. And you will grow in ways that might surprise you. But because you will be well versed in these practices, you will accept it all as naturally as you embrace the inevitability of the rising and setting sun. You will see that your life is like the weather—changeable, unpredictable, sometimes cloudy, sometimes sunny, but always perfect and just as it should be.

EGO

The idea, or rather the reality, of an ego is paradoxical. On the one hand, it gives us a healthy supply of self-esteem, which in turn provides us with the necessary energy to face the world and its inherent storms. On the other hand, it can drive us so deep into self-consciousness that all we can see is ourselves, which leads to a very closed and negative existence. Let's call the first ego our *worthy ego* and the second our *petty ego*.

When our worthy ego is engaged, we cling to nothing, we carry no hate, no fear, no jealousy; we concern ourselves with others and are able to see the larger world and our place in it. When the petty ego is active, our world gets very small; we only care about the world around us insofar as it will give us what we want; we define and relate to everything in the first-person singular, the "I," the "self." This is a very treacherous zone. And until we establish a strong and consistent practice of concentration and mindfulness, it is usually our petty ego that has the loudest voice and the strongest control over us. Our practice here is to distinguish between the two egos and whenever petty ego rises up, notice it and then drop it.

Petty ego is our conditioned mind, and if we remember that everything changes, that nothing is permanent, then we can conclude that ego, too, has no consistent nature, that it is not a fixed phenomenon. This makes it easier to discard when it appears. There is a Zen saying that will help here: *The occurrence of an evil thought is a malady, not to continue it is the remedy.*

Replace *evil thought* with *petty ego*, and you're on your way to creating yourself anew each moment, to not relying on conditioned ego, and to being present in the moment.

True freedom is attained when we gain freedom from the tyranny of our ego, from our desires. When we allow our petty ego free rein, we see ourselves as the center of the universe. When we drop our petty ego, we can see that we are not the center of the universe, but a part of it, and that each part is interconnected and integral to the whole. This automatically leads to unselfish behavior that benefits you and the universe. And this lifts your worthy ego, diminishes your petty ego, and results in a grateful and serene mind.

RELATIONSHIPS

There is probably nothing that challenges us more than our relationships, since every aspect, every nuance of our life involves a relationship of some sort. Every waking and sleeping moment, we are engaged in a relationship with something or someone—with our spouse, boss, children, friends; with coworkers, store clerks, strangers; with our thoughts, dreams, body; and finally with ourselves, our higher self, and our God, whatever that means to you. So in many ways, this area of practice is the ultimate one, the final frontier, the one that we can acknowledge without a second thought is ever changing and never ending. We are never completely alone, for even when any given relationship is not active, there is still a connection with that person. And it is important to remember that our behavior affects those we are in relationship with, and vice versa.

Paradoxically, however, we are alone and solely responsible for our actions.

Here's how the practice of being challenged in relationships works.

- Whenever the behavior of someone else bothers you, turn your focus around, observe your reaction to this person, and ask yourself what it is about this that disturbs you so much, and why.
- Know that you cannot control anyone else—you can be a guide and a teacher and an example, but you can never determine how someone else will ultimately think or behave.
- Practice giving others the freedom to express and be themselves as they uniquely are, without expecting them to conform to your idea of who they are or who you'd like them to be.
- Communicate, communicate, communicate.
- Listen, listen, listen.
- Let the most important human relationship you have be the one with yourself; from there, you will be able to love others.
- Don't take anything too personally.
- Don't take anyone or anything for granted.
- Look to your pets to learn about unconditional love.
- Express yourself. And rather than pointing out to someone that their behavior is bad or wrong, let them know how their behavior affects you. Keep it all on your side of the street.
- Be alert, aware, mindful, caring, generous, forgiving, loving, gracious, and kind to yourself and others, all the time, every moment.

And when there is trouble and discord in a relationship, you might take the following advice from St. Francis: "... *grant that I may seek rather to comfort than be comforted—to understand, than to be understood—to love, than to be loved.*"

Say this or some other favorite prayer each day. And trust that as the above prayer also expresses: *It is by forgiving that one is forgiven.*

FAILURE

Failure is merely a matter of opinion, time, and attitude.

Opinion: Failure is bad. Whenever something happens—especially if it doesn't conform to what society and we think is the optimal scenario—we judge it as bad and look for someone to blame. The one who usually bears the brunt of it in the end is the one who has "failed." For instance, if you were to get fired from your job, even if economic conditions and the state of your company were responsible, chances are that at some point you and others would blame you, especially if some people kept their jobs.

Time: We never know how time will transform events. What is thought of as bad can often turn out to be good after some time passes. Example: After being fired from your job, you go on to pursue the career of your dreams, which would not have happened without the job loss.

Attitude: Keep it positive because you never know. Rather than falling into negative thinking—"I'm no good, I'll never work again, how will this look on my resume?"—engage in positive thinking by seeing the "failure" as an opportunity. For example, "Now I can take that class, start my own business, or change my career focus." When one door closes, another one opens.

When confronted by an event you would normally define as failure, don't be so quick to judge it as bad, let time be the judge, and keep a positive attitude.

Decide that the universe is doing you a favor and helping you create something that you couldn't do on your own. Consider it a gift and it will be. It's another opportunity to practice gratitude.

SUCCESS

In the *Tao Te Ching*, a spiritual text from ancient China, it is written, "Success is as dangerous as failure." This is a succinct way of saying that if we allow either success or failure to carry us away, off the ground, and into a realm of illusion, chances are we'll come crashing down at some point and the fall will hurt. This doesn't mean that if you're enjoying success, you will eventually fail. It means, if you stay grounded, you will maintain your equanimity and be able to accept whatever happens.

These are some of the traps that success can set:

• **Complacency.**
Once we're successful, there is a risk that we will consider our work done and begin to take success for granted. Boredom can be one result, followed by laziness, followed by the disappearance of success.

• **Judgment of others who are either more or less successful.**
To support our insecurities, we might view those less fortunate as inferior and those more fortunate as lucky.

• The "never-enough" syndrome.
No matter how much success we gain, we remain dissatisfied, always wanting more, never grateful for all that we do have.

• Self-aggrandizement.
We boast, we strut, and we gloat, forgetting that success can be taken away as quickly as it was given.

A caution: Watch out for that green-eyed monster of envy and jealousy. When others succeed, be happy for them; congratulate them if you know them, and send good wishes if you don't. Remember, there is plenty of success to go around, and spending your energy on envy and jealousy only depletes you and detracts from your own success. Rather than envying others, try to emulate them. And stick with the winners; spend time with them, learn from them, and love them.

During successful times, this is your practice:

• Continue working with determination.
Allow your goals to be malleable and ever-changing; avoid the trap of thinking that you've made it and reached the end. Life is a dynamic, ever-evolving phenomenon, and so it is with accomplishments. Stay committed to your path.

• Practice charity toward others—in your thoughts and deeds.
When you taste success, be willing to share it. Wish the same for others and help them where you can. Such generosity benefits everyone, and as the saying goes, "In order to keep it, you have to give it away."

• **Call on your worthy ego, not your petty ego, to gain
perspective.**
You deserve success; you worked hard for it. So don't let
your petty ego drag you into stingy thoughts and behav-
iors. Embrace instead your worthy ego or higher self. Be
grateful.

Remember that life is a process and every day brings new
challenges, rewards, joys, and sorrows. With every experience, we learn new things. Nothing is stagnant. This is why
we call it life. So sit, breathe, and move through your life
with energy and determination. If you do, you will know
success.

FRUSTRATION

Indeed, we all have suffered frustration, and sometimes we
let it carry us into a state of anxiety and depression. From
experience, we know that that state of mind never relieves
the frustration; it only aggravates it. Let's take a moment to
look at the most common source of frustration and then how
we might avert it.

Generally, frustration seeps in and takes hold of us when
our needs go unfulfilled and our problems remain unre-
solved. It begins with a desire for something and a craving
for resolution. This wanting is only human. It is our attachment to the outcome that causes us so much discomfort.

When you feel the slightest twinge of frustration, take a
few moments to determine its source. Look again at what it
is that you want, and see if you can notice the real difference
between that and what it is you've been given. Maybe it's simply the same thing packaged differently. Maybe it's something altogether different and something you never could

have imagined. Be open to letting this new thing in and letting go of your original desire. Maybe it's better. Maybe it's just different.

The practice here is not to give up your desire—you are, after all, only human—but to be aware of it and where it takes you. Practice going after what you want and preparing yourself for the manifestation of it, however it comes to you. Be open to all the possibilities. Let go of the ending you've already written for your life. Be present to the way in which your life unfolds without attempting to adjust it to your vision of how it ought to be. What your life has in store for you is even greater than you can imagine, so give yourself over to it. Do the work, and then let go and delight in the wondrous nature of it. Learn to live life on life's terms and frustration will be kept at bay.

DISAPPOINTMENT

Expect nothing. It cannot be stressed too strongly or expressed too often. Expect nothing. If you can simply contemplate these two words and practice them day and night, there's no need to say or do more. Expect nothing.

Something as simple and innocuous as waiting for a promised phone call can lead to disappointment. The caller gets legitimately delayed, you heard the time incorrectly, or there's some other reason the call comes later than expected or not at all, yet you still experience disappointment. When disappointment lingers even after you learn the facts, it may create resentment if you cannot forgive the assumed source of your disappointment. Disappointment can lead to frustration, blaming, anger, and our own bad behavior, so unless we can learn from our disappointment and not react to it, it is best for all concerned to avoid it whenever possible, and, as already stated, the way to this is to expect nothing.

If you're sitting by the phone waiting for the call that doesn't come, your experience might look something like this: You go over in your mind exactly what was said regarding the phone call and determine that you're right, the call is late. You blame the delinquent caller. You get frustrated, worried, angry, and then hugely disappointed. Your expectation is dashed and frustration sets in because you didn't get what you wanted when you wanted it (especially if you weren't engaged in the practice of being still and just waiting).

If you tend to sink into disappointment when something doesn't happen as you imagined it would, were told that it would, or expected it would, then the only antidote is to eliminate expectation. Accept that anything can and will happen, that sometimes the actual outcome will turn out to be even better than anything you could have foreseen, and that you might miss this other, new, and unique scenario if you are sitting with blinders on, stuck in your tunnel-vision point of view.

Know that the stance of expecting nothing takes time to cultivate and much practice to perfect. And also know that it doesn't mean just giving up and becoming a doormat. It simply means that flexibility as opposed to rigidity is called for. You have innate resources to assist you—your breath, your belly-mind, your heart, your intuition, and even your intellect. Call on them all as you face the challenge of being disappointed, and eventually disappointment will be but a tiny blip on your screen of serenity. Changing circumstances will not blow you off your course, you will welcome the unpredictable nature of all things, and you will handle the challenges of your life as smoothly and as gracefully as you sleep. Peace will come if you persevere.

AMBITION

When we practice bringing ourselves into the present moment throughout the day, it can sometimes be very confusing to know how to handle our dreams for the future, our ambitious career and personal plans. If we let our minds take us into this territory, it can get quite tumultuous, indeed. We might ask ourselves such questions as:

- If I'm always in the moment, how can I plan my future?
- If I don't spend time looking ahead to my future, how will I ever achieve anything?
- Isn't it important to look at my past mistakes, the opportunities I missed, and my failed plans, so as to avoid similar pitfalls now and in the future?

The only thing these questions will do is take you out of the present and disrupt your peace of mind. The only thing here you need to know is, if you don't enjoy the process of moving toward something, you'll never enjoy being there, if and when you arrive.

So here are a few tips to help you enjoy your journey:

- Work toward something, but if you're not enjoying your day-to-day activities, rethink your decision.
- Avoid tunnel vision. Don't be so focused on your goal that you miss other opportunities along the way that you would enjoy pursuing.
- Loosen your grip. Allow the dream to change as you change.

- Be flexible. Don't think that there is only one path to achievement.
- Don't cling to your chosen path no matter what—be open to new and different paths.
- Be available to a scenario that you didn't write the script for.
- Always consult your belly-mind when facing a decision.

Ask yourself the following question, which is more about life than about death: *If you knew that you had a short time left to live—six months, a year, two years—how would you spend your days? What would you change, if anything?*

Remember, your life, your future, is happening right now. *This is it!* All you have to do is be present for it. Take a deep breath, fill your whole body with air, and exhale through your fingers and toes. And now settle into your life.

Breathe in and out once more. Repeat this as many times as necessary.

Not only are you right here, right now, but you are also already there.

OPPORTUNITY

Opportunity doesn't always present itself to us as we might expect. It comes in many shapes, sizes, and forms. It can appear when we least expect it and seem absent when we most expect it. It is fickle and unpredictable and yet always available if we're open to it. But due to our habitual patterns, biases, and ways of seeing, we don't always hear it even when it comes knocking loudly on our door. Our internal music is way too loud. Opportunity sometimes appears in the periphery of our vision, but blinders keep it from our view. And our expectations cloud everything.

So, first, turn down the volume, take off the blinders, and

put aside your expectations. Easier said than done? It doesn't have to be. That's a choice. It is a challenge, though, and one that you have to be willing to face. That's all it takes: willingness. The rest is easy. It all flows from that. Endless energy wrapped in determination courses through you when you turn on the tap of willingness.

And then let opportunity court you. Your job is simply to be available and open. Take risks. Some will bring rewards as predicted; some won't. It's the natural ebb and flow of things. The risks you take that don't produce the results you wanted or expected often lead to other choices. Watch out for them. Be alert, be mindful, and be positive.

Remember to keep your balance. Stay centered, focused, and flexible. You have the tools; all you need to do is employ them. If you've already forgotten (it's easy to do, so don't berate yourself), keep in mind that it's all about practice, practice, practice—and progress not perfection.

Usually, we define opportunity as something that, if taken, will benefit us personally. This is basically true, but it's not always as direct as we might think. So, let's look at some of the myriad opportunities that are presented to us every day, ones that carry multiple gifts, like the opportunity to:

- serve others,
- practice charity,
- say nothing,
- just listen,
- practice proper behavior,
- keep a noble silence,
- be tolerant,
- forgive,
- pay attention,

- trust,
- learn, and
- be generous.

And how about these situations that create opportunities for growth:

- an argument with a loved one,
- not getting what you want,
- losing something you have,
- getting what you want,
- the behavior of others, and
- the unexpected.

These lists are endless. Add your own ideas regarding opportunity to them. Be creative. Allow the world in and practice with your heart wide open.

COMPETING AND COMPARING

It's hard not to do it. The world today seems to be all about it. It starts when we're small children and never lets up. The message we get from society is to vanquish all opponents and win no matter what. So competing is just a matter of course, part of the game, an integral part of life. What we may not realize, though, is that it sets us up to compare our skills, talents, and resources with others'. This practice seeps into every aspect of our lives so that we end up constantly looking out at what others do, say, and have—always comparing and being left wanting. Rather than winning anything, we end up losing ourselves and all hope for serenity.

Just as too much thinking causes disquietude and a disturbed state of mind, so too does comparing and competing.

And just as you cannot simply stop your thoughts, you also cannot stop comparing and competing just because you think it's a good idea. With your busy mind and racing thoughts, you learned to invite stillness in by switching your focus to your breathing. With this practice of continually drawing your attention to your breath, deepening your breath, and stilling your body, your mental activity slows down, the silent gaps between thoughts get wider, and serenity begins to settle in. You can use this experience to help you develop a technique that will reduce your comparing and competing tendencies and lead to a higher level of self-esteem, an honorable life, and respect from your fellows, all of which will contribute to your serenity.

The first key to this practice is awareness: Before you can change anything, you must become aware of where you are and what you do. So pay attention. Each time you feel resentment toward someone for what they have, feel "less than" in someone's company, or realize that your focus is completely other-directed, turn your focus around. Without judging yourself for what you're feeling, simply recognize your tendency to compare and compete, notice how it erodes your serenity, and draw your attention back to yourself. Acknowledge yourself for who you are and what you've done, without placing anyone else alongside you. (It is important, though, to recognize and honor those who have helped you and have contributed to your life.) Keep turning your focus back onto yourself. You are no one else, and most likely when you consider the matter deeply, you truly do not want to be anyone else. Draw a sense of gratitude into this self-image. You have your own unique life path, and others have theirs. The longer you spend on your own path and avoid those diversions into others' territory, the stronger you will be, the higher you will hold your head, and the more others will respect you. So, as we touched on before, applaud the success of others, but remain with your two feet firmly planted in your own life. This is where it all will happen for you. Stay put, be grateful, and you will eventually lose the need to compare and compete.

LOVE

We are social creatures and the relationships we cultivate throughout our lives infuse our lives with meaning. Whether or not we express our feelings of love every day to those we love, we know without question who these people are. We could make a list in a minute that would contain our loved ones. Take some time to do that now. The order is not important. Just write a list of all those people you love today. Include those you once loved who are no longer active in your life. This may take more than a minute, but don't think too hard about it. Write from your heart.

If someone comes to mind and you find yourself hesitating to write his name, start a second list of questionable loved ones. Perhaps you're holding on to some anger and don't feel loving at the moment, or you're not quite sure if your feelings toward him constitute love. If he pops into your mind, put him on one of these lists. And if your love of someone has turned to hate, put her on the list as once-loved.

Scan down the first list, the unequivocally loved, and note when you last expressed your love to each person on the list. Make it a point the next time you see them to let them know how much you care. Or if you won't see them anytime soon, communicate your feelings from afar. There are many ways to express love, so be creative. Saying the words "I love you" may be the easy way out. Go out of your way without being extravagant—send a beautiful postcard or their favorite jar of jelly. With those you live with or see every day, make your expressions of love a daily habit without expecting anything in return—give your partner a foot massage, spend an afternoon with your niece. Love simply for the sake of loving.

Now for that second list: This presents a real opportunity to open your heart and love unconditionally. Chances are whoever is on this list has disappointed you or hurt you in some way, has not given you what you need, or has not returned your love in kind. This will be hard, but put aside for now whatever they did or didn't do to you. Decide that whatever it is you want from them will never be forthcoming. Then ask yourself if you still love them. If the answer is yes, then let go of your need to change them or to have them do something that doesn't come easily to them—and just love. Do something nice for them without expecting anything in return. Do something loving without letting them know who did it. And bask in the joy of love.

If the answer is no, then wait a day or two and ask again. If the answer continues to be no, ask yourself if you ever loved them. If they're on the list, chances are the answer is yes, and all that relationship needs is an adjustment. But nothing will change, and your serenity will continue to be compromised until the hate disappears. So embrace this feeling of hate. Draw in hate, and release love. Then reverse it. Draw in love, and release hate. Let the love you feel for all those on your love list overwhelm the hate. As you already know, if hate gets a hold on your heart, there's little room for love and all your love relationships get infected. So embrace the hate and then let it go, and let those sour relationships take their course with only love in your heart.

The Practice of Being Present

When we're disturbed about something, dissatisfied with our life, or simply feeling the blahs, chances are we're thinking about the past or projecting into the future. Too often we live for tomorrow: the anticipated raise, the hoped-for romantic partner or excursion, the time when the kids will be out of the house and on their own. We stare into the future at our plans, hopes, and dreams, confident that the magic elixir, the panacea for our troubled mind and heart, will be there waiting. We continue to live in the delusion that someday our prince will come (or whatever our version of the fairy tale is) and when he does, all will be well, forever and ever, till the end of time.

You don't have to be told that something is wrong with this picture. You might, however, need to be reminded of the alternative—the alternative you sensed is there. You've tasted it—it is always available to you and within easy reach. If you submerge yourself in it, everything makes sense and joy abounds. What is this magical solution? Just this: now, the present, this moment. It doesn't mean that life won't continue to be unfair at times, and unpredictable almost always, but it does mean that if you live in the now, you will know how wonderful life is, even with all its ups and downs.

Joy is only possible when you are in the now. It is not present in the past or in the future. Recall some of your most joyous times, and you'll know the truth of this. You have the chance to live in joy every day, with everyday people, doing everyday things. You needn't wait for the prince. It's not that he's not coming. It's that he's already here.

If you were expecting something grand, something outside yourself, something to sweep you away and carry you into a permanent state of bliss, the news here will be disappointing. But if you can, for just one second, entertain the idea that the truth is even more spectacular than that, then you will know joy, contentment, and serenity in this lifetime.

BROKEN SHOELACES

How many times has a broken shoelace spoiled your morning or whole day? If your first answer is never, because you have no shoes with laces or you've never broken one, keep in mind that broken shoelaces is simply a metaphor for all those little things that happen unexpectedly, always at the wrong time and in the wrong place. These are the things that by themselves cause no harm and have little significance, but that nonetheless impose themselves on us and often interfere with the smooth running of our lives. Spilled coffee, a flat tire, an empty container of milk in the refrigerator—again, a toilet seat left up or down, an unkind word, a red light when you're in a hurry.

I'm sure you can come up with your own list. It would be a good idea to do that right now. Write a list of the little things that have happened lately, even today, that have contributed to altering your mood or your behavior. Then, look beyond the surface. Rather than focusing on the broken shoelace and deciding that if only it hadn't broken you'd be just fine, look past that. First, look at how it affected you. Did you get angry? Did you express or repress that anger? Did you use it as an excuse to do or not do something? Did you blame someone else or even yourself? Avoid justifying your reactions and slipping into your habitual pattern of dealing with things. Do not judge yourself. Simply take notice of the ramifications of the broken shoelace in as detached a way as possible.

Then look more deeply, with no judgment, and see if you can discover why broken shoelaces have the effect on you that they do. Maybe, just maybe, your reaction to the broken shoelace has nothing at all to do with the broken shoelace. If so, take note of the real source. There's no need to do anything. Just pay attention, observe, and acknowledge what it is. Let the truth reveal itself. And then do nothing. Just admit it and sit with it. Breathe it in. Breathe into it. Then move on. And the next time you're faced with a broken shoelace, take a deep breath and remember this little experiment. If you don't catch yourself right away, repeat the above and again look beyond the surface. Do this each time you are faced with a broken shoelace. Before you know it, you will glide right through those once irritating moments. You may still feel the pinch, but you will no longer get tossed around by the unexpected breaking of a shoelace. You will deal with the inconvenience, replace the shoelace, and move on.

If there is nothing beneath the surface of the broken shoelaces, but they keep breaking and disturbing your peace of mind, you have two options: Buy a different brand of shoelaces, or wear shoes without laces.

CHOCOLATE

It is so easy to take the small things in life for granted. Even when we move up to the bigger things, we take them for granted as well. We have much to be grateful for—from hot and cold running water, to toothpaste, to computers and phones. You know this, of course, and you probably also know that you suffer the human tendency to always want more. What you may not realize is that this craving contributes to your discontentment and lack of serenity, and that it will not abate on its own. You must confront it, recognize its hold over you, and then let it go.

Let's say chocolate is one of your favorite treats. You look forward to your midafternoon chocolate break, you reward yourself regularly, and you sometimes overindulge in it. Sometimes it assuages your craving, but many times it does not, so you eat more than you'd like and end up feeling worse. Yet, time after time, you think that it will relieve something, so it becomes a vicious cycle. (If chocolate is not what ignites this insatiable craving, surely there is something else, perhaps money or power? Only you know what it is for you.)

You might think that completely giving up your favorite thing is the answer. Not so, although there are situations where abstinence is the best solution. Usually, all you need to do is pay attention and not expect chocolate to be more than chocolate.

The next time you eat chocolate, be completely present to eating the chocolate. Pay attention to its shape, color, texture, smell, and, finally, taste. Take your time. Breathe deeply as you eat. Notice any impulse to eat quickly or more than you'd like. When your mind moves away from eating the chocolate (and you mindlessly put more in your mouth than you planned), gently draw your mind back to eating chocolate. Introduce a feeling of gratitude into the activity. When you are grateful for chocolate, then gratitude for all other things in your life will follow. After eating your chocolate, write a gratitude list. Head the list with chocolate (or whatever else you are focused on and grateful for at that moment), and remember to include your breath on the list, for without that nothing is possible.

Every time you become aware that you are taking something or someone for granted, take some time out and write down those things you are grateful for. Doing this daily, even without the chocolate, will help you to avoid taking anything for granted. So pay attention to the small things in life, and everything will fall into place.

THE WEATHER

What is it about the weather that can so powerfully impact our moods? We know we have no control over it, yet we often take bad weather—that is, weather that doesn't fit into our plans—personally. We groan and gripe and sulk when it rains on our parade. We let it ruin our day. I doubt there is anyone who hasn't at some point been negatively affected by climatic conditions. We sometimes have difficulty letting rain or cold or heat just roll off our backs. Perhaps the influence is subtle and we don't even associate a gloomy mood with the weather outdoors. Or perhaps it's the indoor atmosphere that unduly disturbs us. We allow the mood and behavior of others to determine our own level of anxiety or serenity.

No matter if it's nature or human behavior, the first thing we must acknowledge is that the atmosphere outside of us is not in our control. We can no more govern how others think and act than we can affect the rotation of the planet. But we do have the power to manage our reaction to the weather. Once we recognize this, we can see that it isn't the weather that determines our mood, it is our reaction to the weather that does. *If it's cold, shiver; if it's hot, sweat.* If it rains when you want sun, change your plans and express gratitude for the rain, which sustains us all. If a drought comes, do your part to conserve water and appreciate that all individual efforts contribute to the whole.

As far as the weather is concerned each day, you must let it do its thing as you do yours. And if you are fully present in each moment and mindfully aware of your actions and reactions, the weather will take care of you as you take care of it.

CHANGE

In New England, people are fond of saying: "If you don't like the weather, wait five minutes." While this is an exaggeration, the fact is that the weather is unpredictable and changeable. Since this quality of impermanence also applies to everything else, we can adapt this saying to our everyday lives: "If you don't like_____, wait five minutes." Fill in the blank.

"If you don't like how you're feeling, what someone is saying, someone's behavior, the crowded streets, the clothes in your closet, or the person you live with, wait five minutes."

You might have to wait a little longer than five minutes, but of one thing you can be sure: In time, something will change. Hence, all the notions regarding time, such as time heals all, time waits for no one, and it's only a matter of time. On the other hand, if you sit around unhappy with the way things are, waiting for them to change, you could wind up hugely disappointed. As an ancient Chinese proverb says: *If we do not change our direction, we are likely to end up where we are headed.*

This tells us that if we want things to change, it's up to us. We cannot usually change the external environment (people's behavior or a crowded street, for example), but we can change our attitude. Adopting a positive attitude leads to positive changes. And remember, before you can change, you must become willing to change.

So why then, if we know that change is inevitable, do we

long so desperately for certainty? Why do we try to lock things into place? Why do we project into the future, and when our lives don't conform to this mental picture, why are we surprised? Perhaps because we want, need, and think we have control. But from our own experience, we all know that we really don't. So your everyday practice here is to accept what is and engage the practice of letting go when you can't. This happens more easily when you admit that the only thing you can be certain of is change, and the only change you can control is change from within.

Then decide what it is that you can change, what it is that you can't, and say the following prayer, by Reinhold Niebuhr, each time your grip tightens around the controls:

> *God grant me the serenity*
> *to accept the things I cannot change;*
> *courage to change the things I can;*
> *and wisdom to know the difference.*

MONEY

Nary a day goes by when we don't make, spend, think, debate, or argue about money. It can be the focus of our obsession, compulsion, greed, anger, or delusion. We may even think it can save or destroy us. We feel good when we have money in our pockets, and bad when we don't. In short, we give it a lot of power. Even saying that money is a necessary evil imbues it with a quality that it doesn't inherently have.

It is not a bad thing to want money, to have money, to spend money. According to Buddha, two of the four things that contribute to our happiness in this world involve money: We should (1) protect our money and (2) live within our means. The other two factors are (3) having good friends and

(4) skill in our profession. Buddha also said that there are four kinds of happiness, of which three are related to money: economic security, freedom from debt, and spending money generously on family and charitably on those in need. But the fourth and most important kind of happiness is spiritual in nature; that is, we should live a good life and not commit evil acts, think evil thoughts, or speak evil words. So even Buddha acknowledged that money is necessary for a happy existence, but if the pursuit of it is our sole purpose, happiness will evade us. We cannot make money our God.

Every day you have an opportunity to experience happiness as you make, spend, and save money. But if you notice that you're placing undue emphasis on it and its rewards, then it's time to pay attention to your spiritual condition. Know that money is a critical ingredient in your happiness quotient, but if your life is not grounded in spiritual practices, then all the money in the world won't matter.

There's really no mystery to what constitutes spiritual practice. Intuitively, you already know what this means. And the more time you spend quietly with yourself listening to your inner voice, the more you will trust your intuition. And then with this pure mind, you will enjoy all the gifts that your money affords.

SEX

First, let's assume that the sex we're talking of here is sex with an appropriate adult partner with whom you have a conscious and loving relationship. In this context, sex is a beautiful and intimate expression of the bond between you and your partner. It is an opening to discover yourself and another in the physical realm. It is also an opportunity to practice trust and letting go, to communicate love in a special way, to be completely in the present moment, and to connect with your partner beyond words.

Contrary to what many people believe, living a spiritually mindful life and sexual satisfaction are not mutually exclusive. In fact, when we are present in every moment throughout the day, we can continue to carry it into the sexual act, which will enhance the whole experience. Approaching sexual relations with an open, honest heart and mindful concentration can be immensely pleasurable.

Just as with other daily activities, bring a sense of ritual and reverence to the act of making love. Have it be a part of your day without the burden of being special. Leave your brain and your ego outside the door of the bedroom, and let the experience of sex be one of heart and body.

If you and your partner are having sexual difficulties, chances are it's not the only area of your relationship that needs attention. Most likely, it is a communication problem. Do not expect sex to solve other issues or for your partner to read your mind. Sex is a way to communicate beyond words, but sometimes the words have to come first. Talk to each other. Take the time to clear up misunderstandings that won't be put aside just by shedding your clothes. If you carry resentments into the bedroom, they will get communicated in one way or another, and will interfere with pleasurable lovemaking. Clear things up as much as possible before sex so that sex can be unencumbered. If you would like something from your partner sexually, bring it up before you are engaged in the act. Communicate what it is you'd like and then let go of all expectations.

Practicing the art of letting go throughout the day in all your activities makes it that much easier to do it during sex, where it is especially important. When we sit with ourselves in silence and delve into our belly-mind, we can say that we metaphorically strip ourselves naked. We let go of the hold our ego has on us and stare into our true nature. In the bedroom, with our love partner, we continue this practice and add the literal act of stripping naked, which places us in a very vulnerable position, indeed. When sitting alone and practicing being still, as thoughts come, we let them come, and rather than holding on or following these thoughts, we just let them go. In the bedroom, we extend this practice to inhibition, fear, and self-consciousness. We notice, we suspend judgment, and we let go of whatever interferes with our being present. With this letting go, we make room for trust—trust in our partner, in ourselves, in love. Trust that there's a shared commitment present and a caring for each other that transcends our petty, selfish desires. When we can let go, trust, and be present like this, two become one. There is no separation; there is true intimacy. Sex becomes a unique experience and one that can inform the rest of our lives. It can give us a taste of what true freedom can mean when we embrace the interconnectedness of all beings.

Love, and allow yourself to be loved in return. Relax, enjoy, breathe deeply; be creative, caring, and unselfish. Simply let go and be present to the joy of sexual union.

The Practice of Letting Go

Whether we plan the major events in our life, such as marriage or graduation, or simply take them when they come, like birth and death, they often cause stress and discomfort, even when the occasion is desired and celebrated. So how do we keep our wits, maintain our serenity, and sail through these times with grace? Simply by relaxing into them. We practice this by keeping our bodies and minds flexible, and we get to this state through the practice of concentration, mindfulness, energy, and joy.

One huge impediment to our serenity when we face the "big stuff in life" is the uncomfortable feeling of not knowing. The only balm for this is letting go. Letting go is easiest when we're in a relaxed state of body and mind.

By all means, do your homework, find out all you can about the circumstances you find yourself in, and take whatever actions are necessary. Be educated. But at some point, you must come to the realization that you can't know the end of the story—how long and happy your marriage will be, when your parents will die, if your career will turn out as dreamed. And at these points, you must let go if you haven't already. Holding on only creates more tension, pain, and suffering. And this produces even more extreme circumstances, which create even more tension, which lead to other conditions, and so forth. The only way to break this progression is to relax and let go of trying to control the outcome. There may be nothing you can do or change about the state of affairs, but you can come to an understanding about it and your reactions to it, which will lead to a more relaxed state, which will help you in the process of letting go. This too is a progression, but a positive one, which leads toward the realization of serenity, even in the midst of chaos.

This may all seem fanciful and impossible to achieve. Not so. Yes, it takes practice. And yes, you may not always be perfect. But if you decide that you are willing to change your usual, habitual patterns of processing the major events in your life (or for that matter, every event in each day), then it will be possible for you to relax, let go, and experience serenity. Practice with the smaller things in life first, so that by the time the big things come around, you will be ready. This new behavior will become so second nature that you won't even have to think about it—a good thing, since there's little time for that when you're facing the big decisions.

Let the future take care of itself by settling into not knowing and relaxing your body and mind. Keep a positive attitude, be mindful of your words and deeds, and embrace your feelings. See things as they are and then let go.

DEATH

It is inevitable that, no matter what our economic or social status is, one day our physical body will die. This is irrefutable. There are a lot of theories about what happens to us—our spirit, our soul, our karma—after we die physically, but no one really knows. And we also do not know when our time will come. Living with this not knowing can cause a great deal of anxiety and fear. Sometimes, without even being conscious of it, we become so afraid of dying that we hold on to life tightly enough to squeeze the life out of it. Afraid of dying, we become afraid of living. In this state, it is almost impossible to overcome our fear of dying. Rather than attack it from that end, let's instead look toward the life end of this spectrum. Let's accept for now that we are only human and that death scares us. Then notice that right now you are alive. Put the thought of death aside for the moment, and trust that today is about life. Celebrate that. Embrace your life. Be grateful for it. And take one small action today that expresses this.

How well do you take care of your body? Do you eat well and mindfully? Do you get enough sleep? Do you exercise regularly? If not, you have some work to do. In your quest for serenity, it is vital that you take proper care of your body. Do not think that a spiritual life of serenity occurs only in the mind. Your body is an integral part of this process. The healthier and more flexible your body is, the healthier and more flexible your mind, and vice versa. There is a symbiotic connection, and this relationship feeds your spirit, which resides in your belly-mind, which sits in your abdomen, which is part of your body. If you take good care of your body and mind, you automatically take good care of your spirit.

One important way to take care of your mind (and by extension, your body) is to carry a positive attitude. Not only does this keep your mind flexible and in synch with your life, but recent clinical studies show that being positive will actually extend your life by as much as seven years.

When your body and mind are relaxed, your desperate hold on life relaxes, and you begin to enjoy life's moments more than ever. Like a strong, deeply rooted tree, you are able to bend without breaking even in the strongest gale.

As the ancient spiritual philosopher Lao-tzu said:

> *The hard and inflexible*
> *are disciples of death.*
> *Thus, the soft and yielding*
> *are disciples of life.*

There are no winners among the rigid.
If a tree won't bend, it will snap in two.

So, live flexibly, centered in your spirit. Take care of your body and mind. Live fully and richly. And you won't be afraid of the unknowable.

ILLNESS

From minor aches and pains to more serious health issues to life-challenging diseases, no one is immune from normal human suffering. But these occasions need not drain your life spirit nor rule every aspect of your life. They can even grant you an opportunity to step aside from your usual existence, take an honest appraisal of things, and reestablish priorities.

The body can often be wiser than the mind. And when we nurture the habit of consulting our belly-mind, we learn the truth of this. But before we become adept in this practice, our body might get our attention by shutting down, which will force us to stop and take a break. This does not mean that all illness is a wake-up call—sometimes a cold is just a cold—but how many times have you fallen ill simply because you needed a break and were unable to take it? How many people do you know, perhaps yourself included, whose lives have been transformed by a grave illness? Whether it's a major or minor setback, sometimes we don't attend to our spiritual well-being until the body breaks down. Here are a few suggestions:

- Take good care of your body; avoid gluttony and the abuse of intoxicants.
- When illness strikes, take the necessary steps to treat the

symptoms and then pay attention to whatever message there might be in it for you.

- When you're ill, be ill. Avoid labeling it as good or bad.
- Be positive. The state of your mental health will affect your physical health.
- Be honest. If falling ill is a means you use to escape the demands of your life, begin looking at other options and what you can do to alter this course. Be brave to be healthy.
- Get the medical help you need, but don't rely completely on anyone else; participate in your own recovery.
- When others become ill, know that you cannot save them. They have their own process. All you can do is offer your loving support.
- Remember the body/mind connection. Eat well, exercise often, and get plenty of sleep.

When you take care of yourself—your body, mind, and spirit—you'll be surprised at how healthy you become, how infrequently serious illness strikes, and how prepared you are when it does. When you take life in stride, even illness won't toss you off the path.

LOSS

Whether we like it or not, loss is a fact of life. What we often don't remember, though, when we're suffering the pain of losing something or someone, is that there is always something gained to set the scales back to balance. We may not notice the gain right away, and it may not appear immediately, but if we keep our eyes and hearts open to this truth, then we need not plunge into the depths of despair when loss visits.

Each year the trees lose their leaves. Each year they return. Even if we have a personal preference for a particular season, we know that no season is absolutely superior to another. They are simply different, with their own unique qualities. Yet even with a phenomenon as unpredictable and changeable as the weather, we can experience sadness when our favorite season ends or when the climate on any particular day doesn't suit us. This is simply the very human tendency to want what we want when we want it. The only remedy for this is to keep a positive attitude, accept whatever comes to us, and know that sooner or later everything changes.

At this juncture, it is imperative to see that while we do have control, at the same time we have none. On our journey into serenity, perhaps this truth is the most difficult to embrace, but it's the most important. The real is not rational and can only be expressed paradoxically. Loss can only happen after we've gained something. And so the reverse is also true. Nothing lost, nothing gained.

While loss may not feel so terrific, keep in mind that it only feels bad because you had something that you thought would last forever, and it's the holding on that causes the pain. So let go, experience the loss, and relax into the natural ebb and flow of life. Sometimes, after some time has passed, the loss itself can be seen as a gain.

There is a common ritual of childhood that helps prepare us to deal with loss—one that we can resurrect and continue to use as adults. Remember the tooth fairy? It helped us as children to learn that a lost tooth wasn't a tragedy and that in good time there would be another. Loss followed by gain. The gift under the pillow simply served as a token to assuage the pain of loss and as a reminder that nothing lasts forever and new growth will occur. We are never too old to be reminded of this lesson. So when something treasured disappears, be your own "loss fairy," and do something to remind yourself that loss is not the end of the story and can be transformed into a gift.

Life may be unfair and it may be unpredictable, but it is also wonderful. And in this wonder, loss becomes one of our greatest teachers. When we respect this, gratitude soars and we reap the benefits of loss as surely as they are there.

BIRTH

The birth of a baby, the birth of a new idea, the birth of a pet project—these are all joyous occasions, full of possibility. So why then do they sometimes hurt so much? Because the true nature of life is paradoxical. Because we're human, we forget and hold on to the idea that good things feel good and last forever, no matter how many times we learn otherwise.

First, understand that every human life contains some difficulties, which in turn cause discomfort, dissatisfaction, and/or outright pain and suffering.

Second, recognize that most of our real discomfort or suffering comes from our desires—for things to be other, different, or better than they are—and our attachments to outcomes.

Third, realize that we can eliminate our suffering by seeing things as they are and letting go of our craving and clinging.

Fourth, follow the path to spiritual wholeness, integrity, and ultimate freedom.

Think of this process as a new birth, a new you. Give up your old ways of handling life, and adopt a new approach. Let go of entrenched ideas, and be open to new ways of seeing. Reach down into your spiritual center, your belly-mind, each time you are confused. The right answer will reveal itself in time. You will know what to do and say when you put your petty ego and pride aside and let your heart and spirit decide. Take time each day to nurture this new outlook. Be mindfully aware of your thoughts, actions, and speech. Take care not to judge yourself or others too harshly. Be patient, yet determined.

Imagine yourself walking slowly through a thick fog. When starting out, you are completely dry. As you move through the foggy mist, you begin to feel damp. Gradually, you get wetter and wetter until you are dripping with a wetness that you cannot even see. So it is as you move through the process of spiritual rebirth. You may not even notice the changes right away. But if you keep on the path, you will eventually become so saturated in this new way of being that you hardly have a memory of your old ways. Just keep walking.

CELEBRATIONS

The unstable trinity of Western holidays: Thanksgiving, Christmas, and New Year's. There's so much to celebrate, yet November to January is the most stressful time of year for many people, contributing to states of depression and anxiety, from mild to debilitating. And then there are all those other occasions we create to celebrate our accomplishments and ourselves—graduations, engagements, birthdays, and weddings—which too often turn out to be more trouble than they're worth. Why do these events, which are meant to elevate and entertain us, compromise our serenity, induce depression, or strain relationships with loved ones? In a word: expectations.

It's one thing to joyfully anticipate a special event; it's quite another to look forward with expectations of how everything will unroll and play out. This is dangerous territory. It always and inevitably leads to disappointment. Not one of us has a crystal ball. No one can predict how things will turn out. Whenever we have a vision of the future in mind, it always turns out to be different. If we're looking for it to be the way we imagined and hoped for, even if it turns out better, we can be disappointed. We may notice the improvement, but we rarely appreciate it.

The solution is to expect nothing. At first, this may seem not only impossible, but also inhuman. If so, take a second look. Practice by living fully in each moment as it comes and in the small daily events. When you notice yourself projecting into the future—even if it's only minutes or hours or days ahead—consciously and mindfully draw your attention back to the moment you are actually in. Use your breath to do it, use your body to do it, use your mind to do it. Completely and gently, guide your expectations into your breath and toward your belly-mind. Fill your belly with your vision of the future as you inhale, and release your hold on it as you exhale. Continue this exercise until there is room in your breath, belly, and mind for whatever will be. Practice this frequently, especially during times of celebration. If you practice this during calm times, you will automatically resort to the practice during times that test your composure. And when the occasion to celebrate is upon you, you will be there for it, in a mood to celebrate.

Then begin to develop this habit: Every time you suffer a disappointment, take some time to trace it back to its origin. Chances are you'll discover it was born of an expectation. The natural progression of this is to eliminate expectations and then reduce disappointment. Then celebrate all the truly wonderful moments of life without any unnecessary baggage. You are the architect of your own life. Celebrate and practice that by being mindfully present in each and every moment, letting go of all expectations.

VACATIONS

Do the planning and preparations for your vacations ever cause more stress than the intended relaxation is able to cure? Do you ever find that you derive more satisfaction from your vacation in the aftermath—telling stories and looking at photos—than in the actual experience of it? Do you so look forward to vacation time that days and weeks go by where you're more in the upcoming vacation than you are in your present day-to-day life, and then when the actual vacation arrives, it is less than you imagined and wanted it to be? Do you live for your vacations and get most of your enjoyment of life from taking time away from your normal routine?

There is nothing wrong with taking a vacation. In fact, it is a very healthy thing to do. But when it interferes with, rather than contributes to, your serenity, you need to ask, what is wrong with this picture? Consider honestly the following statements and which, if any, apply to you:

- I regard vacations as a panacea for my troubles.
- I use vacations to run away from upsetting circumstances in my life, hoping that they'll disappear or be forgotten upon my return.
- I expect vacations to relax and soothe me so that I can return to my life renewed and refreshed.
- I am more truly myself while on vacation than at any other time.
- Vacations afford me the time and space to decide how and with whom I want to spend my life.

Any of these puts an awful burden on the vacation. No wonder it sometimes falls short. Here are some simple suggestions that can help take the pressure off and reinvigorate your vacations with pleasure.

- View your vacation as an extension of, rather than as separate from, your usual life.
- Be wary of any and all expectations attached to vacations.
- Approach vacations as you've learned to do with the rest of your time—mindfully and moment by moment.
- Be open to plans changing at the last minute and to the unexpected. Let yourself get lost.
- The main theme of most vacations is relaxation, one form of letting go. If you practice this way of being in your day-to-day life, you'll be prepared when your vacation rolls around. When you return, you'll be renewed and refreshed.

JOB LOSS

"I heard the news. Congratulations. Terrific! Wonderful! What a stroke of luck."

If you lost your job and someone said these things to you, would you think they were

(a) uncaring and insensitive, or

(b) wise and perceptive?

The normal, conventional choice would be (a), and (b) would seem not only preposterous but also cruel. Yet (b) is the better choice, and here's why: We never know how events will unfold, and we limit ourselves when we view the world in dualistic terms—for example, losing job is bad; keeping a job is good.

Invariably, when one is "relieved" of one's job, the knee-jerk reaction is fear. There may be lots of other emotions mixed in as well—such as anger, shame, or relief—but fear colors them all. Even if we dislike our job and often wish it away, if it is taken from us, we tend to keep holding on. We want to know what's next; we grasp after security and certainty. We panic when we lose what we thought was secure and worry about how we'll feed our family and pay our bills. Some of the practical matters, like temporary loss of or reduction in income, are serious, but there is always a solution, which we can't see if we're in a state of panic. The simplest solution to the immediate financial crisis (which most of us focus on as the *big* problem) is to ask for help to get through the short term. Help is always available in some form, though pride often blurs our vision and erects such a huge barrier that we often don't even realize it's right there in front of us.

Is there security and certainty inherent in any job? No, not really. Can the loss of our job ever be a good thing? Yes, nearly always. If we cling to our job and delude ourselves by thinking that the security and certainty (however false) are worth whatever displeasure our job creates, we limit our choices. In this state of fear, if we are relieved of our job, we are not prepared for the subsequent emotional turmoil. It can then be difficult to take advantage of the opportunity that losing a job offers us. Losing a job (regardless of the reason) can grant us some free time to spend assessing what it is we want to do next in our lives. It can be a gift that we wouldn't have given to ourselves that allows us to pursue a long-buried dream. It can be the kick in the butt we needed to make a change that deep in our heart we knew was inevitable. It can be the wake-up call we were waiting for that will help us transform our work life into a meaningful affair.

It can signal the end of a life half-lived and the beginning of a life fully realized.

Think of being fired as something that the universe is doing for you that you couldn't do for yourself. Resist the impulse to blame and recriminate. Breathe in your fear and breathe out courage. Trust that even if you loved what you were doing, there is something more magnificent awaiting you. Continue to tell yourself that this is a precious opportunity, not to be wasted—the chance in a lifetime that not everyone is given. Each time negativity appears, take it in and turn it upside down. Flip that coin on its tail. You've been given some time, so take it; don't rush toward the answer. Time takes time, and when it's time, you will know what to do and how to proceed toward the only possible positive next step for you. Be brave, even as you feel afraid. This is when the journey can get positively exhilarating and you can become fully engaged in the moment-to-moment movement of your life. Don't allow a little thing like fear to rob you of this growth opportunity. *Carpe diem!* (Seize the day!)

The Practice of Being Aware

It is in the arena of feelings that most of us get tossed around unwittingly. Sometimes feelings (especially those we label as "negative") can be so powerful that we let them rule our lives. We tend to resist and push away the feelings we don't want and hold on tightly to those that we wish would last forever. Even though experience teaches us that neither approach is effective for maintaining serenity, we continue to behave in this way because it seems to make sense to us. We push away that which we don't like and hold on to that which we do. In this section, you will learn about practices that seem counterintuitive—that is, embracing the feelings that you want to be rid of and letting go of those you want to keep.

What we are aiming for is balance, equanimity, and evenness of mood. What our habitual thinking tells us to seek is happiness ever after, endless joy, and eternal bliss—especially if we read fairy tales as a child. We believe in these childhood promises, even though we know that everything changes, that nothing is permanent. It's not that joy isn't available to us— it most definitely is. But if we want to live in a state of serenity, we must view the world realistically and accept that a full life contains all feelings, good and bad. Our job is to live in the paradox of reality and know that we are more than our feelings, that whatever our feelings in any given moment, they'll eventually pass, and that we have the power to transform our feelings.

For every feeling, there is an opposite feeling. Would we even know joy without suffering? Hope without despair? Anger without compassion? Surely most of us would rather there be only one side to the feelings coin (the "good" side), but obviously this isn't possible. So, for now, as you work with the practice of feelings, put aside your dualistic measure of things and refrain for the time being from judging anything as good or bad, right or wrong. Be open to a new way of looking at things. Turn your usual point of view upside down and inside out. Let go of the need to know before you know. Then you'll be ready to explore and live in a state of well-balanced self-assurance, where no feeling will seduce, overwhelm, or control you. Composure under all conditions will prevail and serenity will be yours.

PAIN

This may be the one overriding feeling that we'd all like to avoid, be it of the physical, mental, emotional, psychological, or spiritual variety. But there is no life without pain. Even in birth, the most spectacular and miraculous event in life, there is pain. Yet even when we accept that pain is a part of life and unavoidable, we still go to extreme lengths not to feel it. Here is an exercise that you can do daily that will help you understand your relationship to pain and teach you to manage all sorts of pain. If you persevere, you will discover that pain can be your friend.

Begin by sitting completely still for ten minutes a day, and build up to forty minutes once you establish a practice. Keep your spine erect. Begin in as comfortable a position as possible, with no overlapping, interlaced arms, legs, or fingers. Concentrate on your breath. Keep your eyes open. Don't move. No matter what, don't move. If you get an itch, don't scratch it. If your leg falls asleep, let it be. If you think of something that you must do right away, stay seated and continue breathing. The itch will fade, your leg will eventually wake up (and there will be no permanent damage, no matter what your mind tells you), and the chore that needs doing will be waiting for you.

As you sit, notice your resistance (which is, by the way, normal). Watch how this resistance can intensify the pain. Practice breathing into whatever pain comes up and just letting go. Use your breath to manage your physical pain. Observe yourself—your reactions, thoughts, feelings, impulses, and projections vis-à-vis your pain. And do nothing. Just keep sitting through it. Whenever you become aware of being in pain, change the thought of "I'm in pain," to "pain." Take the "I" out of it. See the pain simply as pain, nothing more.

Here are some things you might experience and learn about physical pain if you practice this exercise daily:

- All pain passes (or at least changes).
- The thought of future pain can intensify current pain.
- Resistance to pain accentuates it.
- It is never as bad as we think it is.
- Accepting it and breathing into it lessens the impact and often releases it.
- Wanting it to be something other than what it is makes it worse.
- We create some pain merely for the entertainment value.
- Over time, with practice, it gets physically easier to sit still for the allotted time.
- We become better able to handle painful situations when not doing sitting-still practice.

If you practice sitting with pain, then whenever pain arises, on whatever level, you will intuitively know what to do with it. Each time pain pays a visit in any area of your life, you will reach for the techniques you honed while sitting still to help you. You will see how pain is often just an illusion that disappears in due time as long as you don't hold on to it. You will also realize that pain is a normal part of human existence and that suffering with it is optional.

Pain is one of our greatest teachers. Make friends with it, and let it instruct and guide you toward greater clarity and purpose.

NEGATIVITY

There may be nothing that interferes with serenity more than a negative attitude. Not only that, a negative attitude can be detrimental to your physical, mental, and emotional health. It's a vicious cycle. The only thing that can break this cycle is to adopt a positive attitude, no matter what.

The popular epigram known as Murphy's Law, "If something can go wrong, it will," points to how endemic negativity is, not to mention easy. But think about this: If it's so easy to predict and create negative situations, why can't it be just as easy to turn that around and replace the negative with the positive? Well, it is that easy. All it takes is awareness, a decision, and an action, which will lead to change in habitual patterns, which will create space for new, positive habits to develop.

No matter what the external landscape in any given moment happens to be, remember that you have the power to choose your mental environment. The first thing to do is to become aware of your negative thinking. If you are displeased in any way, chances are you're thinking in a negative fashion. Don't judge—just notice. Then decide that you want to reverse this manner of thinking and that changing it is up to you. Own the negativity. Breathe it in. And then breathe out being positive. Keep doing this until you notice a shift. You may have to practice it throughout the day if you're having a particularly difficult day or if a negative outlook is deeply ingrained in you. Don't give up. If you continue this practice and keep the clear intention that a positive attitude is truly what you want, then you will replace a negative view with a positive one.

Keep in mind the law of cause and effect. Negative thoughts and actions create negative results. Being positive creates positive results. But watch out for those expectations. Being positive doesn't mean that everything will go your way and that you will get everything exactly as you want it. Simply be positive and let go. Holding on is about fear, which is the mother of all negative attitudes. So use your greatest gift, your breath, to help you establish trust in letting go. Breathe in being positive. Breathe out negativity. While it may seem counterintuitive, it also works the other way. Breathe in negativity; breathe out being positive. Try it, and just keep breathing.

HOPE

Have you ever made any of the following comments? What do they have in common with each other? How do they get you in trouble?

- Let's hope that never happens again.
- Let's hope for the best.
- If only I could _____, I would _____.
- Imagine how nice it would be if _____.
- There's always hope.

Instead of saying: I wish this war would end and peace would come.
Ask: What can I do to achieve harmony in my life today?

Instead of thinking: I hope he finds his way.
Ask: What can I learn from his experience?

Instead of thinking: I hope I get that job.
Ask: What can I do today? What am I doing today?

Hope is something that we all call upon when the going gets rough. While I'm not the first to say it and it may sound blasphemous, try this instead: Give up all hope.

What does hope accomplish other than taking us out of the moment, projecting us into an unforeseeable future, and building up our expectations? What is hope but a desire for change, a wish for circumstances to be other than what they are?

It's not wrong to hope to get better, for instance; it's just not a good idea to live solely in that hope. Bring yourself into this moment and be completely present. Deal with whatever is right in front of you now. Pay attention to the sound of your breathing. Admire the abundant colors all around you. Be grateful for your life as it presents itself to you.

When we give up all hope, we can't help but be right here, right now. And only when we are in the present, do we have the opportunity for peace of mind, serenity, and true contentment. Being present allows us to appreciate the gifts in our life and marvel at the way life moves.

Life is unfair. Life is unpredictable. And though you may think you'd be happier if you could call all the shots and make things happen to suit you, if you sit still long enough and listen to your deep truth, you will know how false this is. What choice do you have but to accept the unpredictability of life, go with the flow, and see how wonderful your life already is?

So, whenever you notice yourself hoping for something different, breathe into your belly and out through your toes. Feel the air enter your nostrils and follow it as it fills your lungs and expands your rib cage, diaphragm, and belly. As you slowly release the air, feel your body relax into itself. Breathe in peace. Breathe out hope.

You can also try this another way: As you inhale, breathe in all the hope that you and others you know are feeling. Think of all those in dire circumstances and breathe in the hope that they must be holding on to. Then breathe out peace. Think of all those people receiving this peace that you are exhaling into the universe.

Try it both ways whenever you reflexively begin to hope. Train this new muscle that you are developing and breathe away hope. It might take some time, but before too long, your outlook will shift and be more consistently positive. There's no need to hope. It's as simple as that.

JEALOUSY

It's so easy to look at the behavior of others to justify our feelings. But no matter what other people do or say, we are ultimately responsible for our own feelings. You could probably convince anyone who will listen that another person's behavior is deplorable and it's natural for you to feel the way you do. But isn't that giving them all the power over how you feel? How does giving away your power affect you?

Can you do something to reverse that? Without my saying so, of course you know that you can. Intuitively, you know that only you are responsible for how you feel.

Jealousy is a tricky one. Often, it is precipitated by a loved one acting inappropriately and not considering your feelings, or by an imagined indiscretion, or by comparing, or wanting, or coveting. More often than not, we create scenarios in our mind to feed this green-eyed monster. Usually, it has little to do with the truth, the real circumstances. Mostly it has to do with the fear of losing something or someone we want—a case of our petty ego taking control. And our self-esteem is often at issue whether we realize it or not. Because we're so intent on watching and imagining the antics of others, we cannot even see ourselves in the picture.

So the first thing to do when jealousy rears its ugly head is to do an about-face and look in the mirror at yourself. Investigate the source of the feeling. Divorce it from the current target. See how far back it goes. Then admit that at the core of the jealous feeling is love. Focus on that. See how fear gets into the mix to disguise and obscure the truth. Keep focusing on the love. Express those love feelings to the person who has aroused the jealousy. Take a risk. Express yourself, your truth, your love.

Don't expect anything in return. Luxuriate in the pure nature of giving. Withhold nothing. Spend it all. When you do this, love will come back to you tenfold. It may not come from where you're looking, so be prepared and open and available for anything. Don't lock yourself into any corners that you can't move out of. Open your heart wide, and love, not jealousy, will be your reward.

MOODS

Some people wake up naturally each morning in a sunny disposition, immediately ready to greet the day. Others struggle with moodiness first thing and need time to sort themselves out before facing whatever awaits them. There are morning doves and there are night owls. Which are you? We might get it in our heads that one temperament is preferable to another, that one is better, superior, the one to aspire to. This is again just our black-and-white outlook operating, which requires us to define some things as good and their opposites as bad. This dualistic point of view does us a huge disservice. The first thing to do here is to suspend judgment, so that we can see clearly without the cloud of guilt that usually hangs over the moods we've categorized as bad.

Even when we adopt a positive attitude toward life, there will still be times when we'll feel sad or lonely or discontented or just plain dull—moods that we've been programmed to define as bad. But if we can remove that label and just allow ourselves the emotion, whatever it is, we can then get in touch with a valuable piece of ourselves that needs expression. And when we do this, we're less likely to wallow. If we repress "bad" feelings, they sometimes force themselves on us; since we're unused to feeling them, we may not even know how to describe them when they do surface. It's important to allow all feelings, because repressed feelings only end up causing dysfunction and ill health in the end. Let the feelings come, identify them, let them run their course, and let them move on.

You may find that as you awaken to the whole range of feelings, those you once considered bad may redefine themselves as good, and vice versa. For instance, expressing sadness about a lost relationship might bring you closer to a current one. Articulating your feelings enables you to put them behind you and live more fully in the gifts of the present. Regret disappears and love blossoms.

When we are in close touch with how we're feeling at any given moment, and when we embrace whatever feeling is there, we have the best chance for maintaining our equanimity. No one feeling gains prominence, we spend less time on the extremities of the feelings spectrum, and we reside smack in the center of who we are—without shame, guilt, apology, or superiority. It's about balance, about being human, and about reserving judgment.

FEAR

More than anything else, fear can interfere with our having a serene and fulfilling life. It can keep us from doing those things that we most want to do and being with those we most cherish. It can rule our life if we let it. Even when we become aware of its power, we still gravitate toward it and quite simply choose to let it have reign over us. Fear can be a familiar and comfortable place. It seduces us because it is predictable and grants us the illusion of control. It also helps us keep the mystery of things, people, and places alive. We believe that if there's no fear, there's no mystery.

By confronting your fears, you can overcome them. It's likely that you're not even in touch with what scares you, so identifying your fears is the first step in the process. Begin by making a list of everything you feel afraid of, from simple everyday matters to the larger, more complex issues of life. Your list might include some of the following:

· Roller-coaster rides
· Airplanes

- Social gatherings
- Failure
- Success
- Ridicule
- Intimacy
- Being wrong
- Rejection
- The unknown
- Realizing your dreams

At the core of all fear is the fear of disappearing, of annihilation, of not being accepted, understood, or loved. This all adds up to the fear of dying. It is only human to have this fear. The problem is that, too often, it keeps us from truly living. We must stop running from ourselves, stay put, and give expression to our fears. Naming begins the process of rendering our fears powerless. It gives us enough courage to investigate the fear, sit with it, and do the opposite of what it would have us do.

You are not your fears. You are also not responsible for having the fear. All you need to concern yourself with is your reaction to fear. When you face fear and decide to not let it control you, the subsequent actions result in greater self-esteem, a sense of accomplishment, renewed vitality, and freedom. Fear then begins to recede. It loses its grip on you when you don't let it take hold.

Fear may never disappear completely—after all, we are only human—and it can take on a subtlety that can surprise us. But in time, when we take on our fears, our joy of living grows exponentially, death becomes just another life event, and the mystery of life continues.

JOY

Such a small word for such a big feeling! How often have you used this word to describe your mood? Are you one of those people who hold it in reserve for special occasions, for the grand moments of life? There is so much pressure to have everything perfect before we employ this word to describe how we're feeling that we hardly ever use it.

If you want to experience more joy in your life, begin to notice how you verbally express your feelings. Are you more skilled at describing negative, painful feelings than positive, joyous ones? Whether this is true for you or not, start to pay attention to the small details throughout this day that impart a feeling of happiness, no matter how minute they might be. Your morning cup of coffee, an op-ed column by your favorite writer, a fresh, juicy orange in the middle of the afternoon—mark these experiences as moments of joy. Take the time to savor the feeling, without expectation, projection, or comparison. Let it be what it is—in the moment that it is.

Sometimes we take for granted the small moments of joy that occur each day and let the more disturbing feelings, which may also reside in each day, color our overall mood. This can lead us to believe that we are generally discontented, causing us to wish and hope and dream for a more joyful existence. We think of joy as something to attain, to aspire toward, something that someday will be ours, permanently. But there's no need to wait. There are joy moments in every day for each of us. We simply have to notice them, name them, and be in them. By doing this, we will bring a sense of balance to the day, and then, by extension, to our whole life.

In everyone's day, in each of our lives, there are good times, there are bad times; there are joyous moments and sad moments. If we participate in our life, take things and feelings as they come to us, without unfairly judging or getting swept away by any of them, we can create a life of equanimity. Thus, joy will be a part of every day. We will no longer have to wait for the *big* feeling of joy. It is there for us to have any moment, anywhere. No big deal. And yet a very big deal, indeed.

ANGER

Plays have been staged around it. Volumes have been written about it. Wars have been waged because of it. Relationships have disintegrated, health has been compromised, and serenity has been lost altogether. All of this has been in the service of anger. And what is it but a reaction to the way things are and a desire to have them otherwise? More often than not, anger is triggered in our relationships with others. We rail at their behavior and treatment of us because we know a better way, the right way, to behave. Often it has nothing to do with us. Mostly our anger derives from our self-centered fear. When things don't go as we want them to, or think they should, we become afraid of disappearing. Our defense is anger, followed by some attempt to manipulate circumstances to our liking. Experience tells us that this doesn't work, but we continue to react with anger out of habit.

There is another way. That way is acceptance, compassion, and love—of yourself and others. This is where your self-centeredness can work for you. Decide that you are as important, not any more or less, as those around you. Don't repress your anger, but before you expose it to others, take a good look at it. You may find that your anger is justified. Even so, ask yourself if it will serve any useful purpose. The answer is always no if you're honest with yourself and you don't let your petty ego and pride interfere. So rail silently, and express your anger in writing and perhaps to a confidante. Then let it go. For if you let it hang around, the only one it will destroy is you.

Practice acceptance. This does not mean to be passive. Take action against situations that exist to exploit others, for instance. Use your anger in a positive way. Do what you can and then let go. Use your breath to help you stay in the moment. If you are present to the immediate moment, there will be no anger, because the past, future, and even the present will disappear. Then love will have a chance—the only cure for anger.

Each time you become angry, stop and take a look at it. Usually, we just let it take charge without even noticing it. So paying attention is the first step toward conquering it. Sit silently with it and observe your anger, without judgment. Rather than saying, "I'm angry," just notice that there is anger. Watch how anger arises and how it disappears. In fact, you can do this with all your emotions, and by so doing, become the detached observer of your own mind.

When you know your mind, you will know yourself. No matter what the circumstances, it is up to you to choose your own mental and emotional environment—one that doesn't honor anger, we hope. This is ultimate freedom and true serenity.

Closing Thoughts

CURIOSITY

When we stop resisting and struggling against the parts of our life that we believe we can't abide, and instead investigate our reactions, attachments, thoughts, and feelings, we have a greater chance of achieving and living in serenity. Whenever you are confronted with something that bothers you, practice not shrinking from it. Engage the curiosity that brought you to pick up this book and others like it to look inside yourself and see what's there. Anytime you become aware that you are searching outside yourself for answers, turn your focus around and look within. By all means, read spiritual literature, attend lectures, and research what the masters throughout history have had to say about leading a spiritually serene life. Then take what you learn and draw it into your body, into your belly-mind, and filter it all through your intuitive personal truth. See how it fits. Be discerning. Trust yourself.

If you're in crisis, seek outside help, and let trusted others take care of and help make decisions for you, and when you are comfortably back to normal, begin to renew trust in yourself.

When Buddha was near the end of his life, some of his students asked him to impart to them some final words of wisdom, something that they could hold on to after he was gone. They were still dependent on him, so he gave them the greatest teaching of all. He said, "Be a lamp unto yourself." This is inspiring advice and as appropriate now as it was 2,500 years ago. What he meant by this is to rely on yourself, not on others. Rely on the "truth" of life, the truth that your belly-mind, your intuition, your "gut" imparts to you. Trust in this truth. Investigate this truth. Look toward others, and learn what you can from them, but in the end, decide for yourself what works best for you. By looking into your heart and belly-mind—while keeping pride and ego at bay—you will find all the answers you seek.

Here is a short list of some things you can sit with, contemplate, and meditate on as you progress on your journey.

- What hindrances do I encounter that rob me of serenity, such as ill will, worry, or doubt?
- Who is the "I" that thinks my thoughts or feels my feelings?
- What is mindfulness exactly?
- How does desire help and hinder me?
- Can love and compassion really conquer all?

Sit with your mind, study it, and know it—without judgment or criticism. Be curious about how it works. Delve into your belly-mind. Practice breathing in and breathing out that which pains you and that which comforts you. Let this practice develop into a daily habit and evolve into a meaningful spiritual practice.

When you take the time to quiet your chattering *monkey mind* (a Buddhist term that describes our unsettled, busy, restless mind that keeps us away from inner peace), sit still for a few moments, and listen to your "true nature," you will undoubtedly know right from wrong, you will know what next action to take, and when to do nothing. You will learn how to be at peace in your life, which will lead you to be completely awake for whatever life serves you. Your life will then not simply be about your life. It will be about giving your life to be of service to others. And in this giving, you will truly be born, again and again, moment by moment. Thus, you will have serenity in motion—inner peace, anytime, anywhere.

Index

ABOUT THE AUTHOR

Nancy O'Hara is the author of six books on the subject of mindfulness and meditation. Along with her writing, she shares her experience through her Zen Life Coaching practice, meditation classes, private and corporate workshops, and retreats. Nancy lives in New York City. For further information, see her web site www.samumeditation.com.